OUT AND ABOUT

Reflections on nature
and some of the rest of us

C. P. Stone

Artwork by

Jeff Kitterman

Out and About
Copyright © 2010 by C.P. Stone

Layout
    IRIS Enterprises
    Eveleth, MN

Published by
 Shadow IRIS Books
    IRIS Enterprises
    4451 Lakeside Drive
    Eveleth, MN 55734-4400
    www.speravi.com/irisbooks

Printed in USA

Artwork by Jeff Kitterman

Library of Congress Control Number: 2010922278

ISBN: 978-0-9796562-3-1

1. Nature   2. Minnesota   3. Poetry

Comments on OUT AND ABOUT

"These easy-reading poems reflect [a] deep and gentle respect for nature . . . [they] give us insight into a connected lifestyle and expand our knowledge of the natural world"

> Gary Stone, photographer, long-time resident of northern Minnesota, Ely, MN

"A very broad, expansive [book] sharing deep thoughtfulness . . . You might consider doing an audio edition"

> Andrew and Elizabeth Urban, retired English teacher, nature lovers, residents of northern Minnesota, Ely, MN

"Good expressions of life and love of place . . . [I] could really experience the natural world through your senses – all of them – sight, sound, smell, taste, touch, being"

> Suzanne Fellows, wildlife biologist, environmental educator, author, Lakewood, CO

"Detailed poetic observations described with a deep sense of caring and love . . . You have written an exceptional piece of literature"

> Roger and Kathy Weaver, theologian, nature lovers, residents of northern Minnesota, Tower, MN

"The book brings alive our experiences with nature . . . The [author's] knowledge and love of nature show"

> Lowell and Betty Snyder, outdoor enthusiasts, Waverly, IA

"With a scientific eye and a poet's heart, the author shares his unique observations on the world of nature . . . His lyrical wisdom is sure to increase biological awareness and awaken the slumbering poet that resides in us all"

> Mary Kay Kilgannon, freelance writer/editor, Lakewood, CO

"The poems within offer texture and detail to familiar landscapes, as well as experiences of quiet beauty here in the North Woods . . . I love . . . the word pictures, your appreciation for nature, remembrances, as well as your wry sense of humor"

> Gloria Gervais, retired teacher, long-time resident of the North Woods and naturalist wannabe, Ely, MN

"I hope [the book] will engage appreciation [and] promote understanding of the values of wise use . . . It has the makings of a remedy to *The Last Child in the Woods*"

> Bill Tefft, college instructor, naturalist, radio show host, Ely, MN

For my wife Danny
Like me, a resident alien of several cultures

ACKNOWLEDGEMENTS

I appreciate very much the generosity and insightful comments of reviewers of this effort. Many commented in writing or orally on most of the poems, and on the work as a whole. Reviewers included: Suzanne Fellows, Gloria Gervais, Mary Kay Kilgannon, Lowell and Betty Snyder, Danielle Stone, Gary Stone, William Tefft, Andrew and Elizabeth Urban, Roger and Kathy Weaver and Steve Wilson. Some of their comments appear in the front of the book and on the back cover.

Thanks to Charles Morello of IRIS Enterprises, publisher and advisor on many technical matters, including design and layout. I enjoyed working with Chuck, as usual. David Schmidt, Wolfland Computers, also helped with computer questions.

Danielle Stone read several drafts of the manuscript, made many suggestions, and identified a number of problems. I am grateful for her support and encouragement during the writing process, and for her companionship in many of the outdoor activities described.

Jeff Kitterman was a pleasure to work with on illustrations. He not only produced excellent artwork in a timely fashion, but also provided CDs scanned in the proper format for publication. Candy Ronning, *Sauk Centre Herald*, scanned the artwork and colorized the cover.

CONTENTS

SUBJECTS OF ARTWORK

INTRODUCTION

Outdoor recreation is a favorite pastime of many people. "Consumptive" outdoor activities, such as hunting and fishing, usually have the primary goal of physically taking something away from the experience, for example, food or trophy. "Nonconsumptive" recreation, such as walking or biking, skiing or snowshoeing, canoeing or kayaking, does not have the goal of physically removing something from the outdoors. Both kinds of outdoor recreation can lead to release from stress, "re-creation" of attitudes and viewpoints, social interactions, physical exercise, sunshine and fresh air, spiritual thoughts and feelings, and close rapport with nature. Group traditions, self esteem from doing something well, and a change of scenery are among other benefits.

I believe that connection with nature is more important than many of us make it, for additional reasons. Without outdoor experiences, there is not much chance of understanding and being well-informed about the world around us. A number of phenomena related to nature can only continue or increase in the 21st century. Among them: Increasing numbers of people and outdoor recreation, expanding materialism, water and energy shortages, deforestation and desertification, storm and wildfire frequency and severity, food shortages, extinction of species, spread of alien (introduced) species, and global climate change. These and other problems cry out for informed decision-making about the natural world and our effects on it. If more people intentionally connect with nature in meaningful ways, better decisions should be possible, area by area, region by region, and worldwide. Such decisions are not merely matters of economics; reasoning based only on simplistic and readily available information about costs are used far too frequently in our society.

Dedicated natural areas such as national and state parks and forests, refuges and preserves, and wilderness areas are critical places to connect with the outdoors. Most have been set aside to protect biological communities from development or from other destructive effects of expanding human populations, at least in part. These areas are relatively stable due to legal mandates, and they can often support species that require considerable space. However, close-at-hand, smaller areas, if used with intention, can also provide important connections with nature for most people.

One key aspect of intentional interaction with the natural world is a focus on awareness. By this, I mean more than identification of what plant or animal is encountered, although that is an important first step. One can also pay attention to *phenology* (changes related to weather and seasons); more than one *taxon* (group, such as birds or plants); *ecology* (relationships among taxa); and *conservation* (protection and management of nature). When does a species of plant flower or set seed? When does a species of bird arrive and depart? What affects the abundance and distribution of plants and animals in an area? For species that are not present year-round, where are they when they are away? What might affect them in other areas? Which plants and animals are found together? Which insects eat other insects or plants? What activities of humans seem to impact the plants and animals observed?

Slowing down enough to observe, to question, to wonder, is key. This does not come easily to many of us used to instant gratification from electronic gadgets, or to those of us involved in fast-moving and hectic jobs. Allowing time to identify, raise questions, and take notes or pictures for further thoughts later can lead to deeper understandings. Looking things up on the Internet or seeking out books or people to help can increase knowledge and interest.

But won't a more thoughtful approach take away from enjoyment of the outdoors? Isn't being outside largely a matter of not doing much of anything? We are human *beings*. Why do we always have to be *doing* things? Why can't we just relax and kick back?

I suggest that what we do helps shape our being. Certainly we all have to choose (by default, if nothing else) how much "free" time we spend outdoors, helping others, being activists for one cause or another, planning menus, following the stock market, caring for our possessions, or sitting in front of a blue screen. What we choose to be aware of and what we value are reflected in what we do. What are we passionate about or connected to? How do we spend our non-work time? What isn't getting done because of what is? Of course, some of us value a meaningful connection to nature more than others. But most of us are losing what will be a vital link to problem-solving and to our own identities in the future.

However you choose to spend your time, I wish you success in your efforts. Being outdoors and deliberately doing things there has helped me improve both intention and awareness. Reflecting on and writing about outdoor experiences has also been a source of satisfaction.

Someone has said that poems and short stories are perfect forms of written communication for our time – suited to an age when we are all in a hurry. I have chosen to use poems to try to convey thoughts and feelings about some of my experiences outdoors. Perhaps they will help someone else connect to nature. I hope you have many slow, meaningful and continuing experiences of your own in the natural world around you. Enjoy!

WINTER

ICE-UP TIME

Fragile skim ice floats near the shore
As we approach the lake
The water open clear across
Wind's ripples in its wake

The sky snowed twice, bright glistening shards
And before we knew it
The whole lake white with fallen snow
Winter freshness to it

Then shone the sun, the ice came clear
Of snow in winter's light
The wind had not begun to play
The ice was smooth and bright

Thin skim ice tinkled near the shore
Breaking in pieces fine
Pushed inward by sheets farther out
Over the course of time

Then blew the wind to rumple up
The surface of far ice
Skating after thickening progressed
Would not now be so nice

Lake ice began to moan and crack
As it fit to the shore
Contract, expand, both out and back
The water was no more

Then came deep snow and drifted in
Water pushed up through cracks
Ridges soon formed where forces met
Before sun's warmth came back

Now deep snow and some slush protect
The ice layer underneath
Hardening and thickening slow apace
Cold air cannot quite reach

But soon mid-winter's lows are here
And ice that's fit for use
Till then, those who use frozen lakes
Find safer things to do

WINTER BIRD SOUNDS

The hoar frost shines on shrubs and trees
The sun comes up to look at me
Air so brisk I can see my breath
Some would say it is still as death

But birds are in this quiet place
A downy hammers, strong tail braced
Chickadees call out in their flocks
They dash around, their tails half-cocked

And soon nuthatches start their noise
"Yank yank," two pitches, girls and boys
The raven "quorks" as it flies by
He'll nevermore soprano try

A pileated's cry rings out
No flickers now, so there's no doubt
No other sound so loud and shrill
Could issue from these snowy hills

Yes, blue jays shriek a bit, it's true
One cries out "thief," as if it's you
Not like the gray jay's soft, pure sound
Caressing ears now all around

Winter bird sounds go with the stark
The cold and wind and semi-dark
And year-round birds that stay the course
Deserve respect, better or worse

Though not a springtime symphony
Winter bird music pleases me
The birds that stay north all year long
Do sing their own endearing song

THE WINTER OF *THEIR* DISCONTENT

"The winter of our discontent"
I never knew just what that meant
Is it a phrase from the far north
From one who dares not venture forth?

Or is it from someone down south
Who has no cold weather to tout?
Who lives in warm and humid air
And realizes it's not fair

Who never has to haul firewood
To heat a home warm as one should
Who doesn't have to use heat tape
To keep the water lines in shape

Poor soul, without windows and doors
Well insulated, heated floors
Who lacks storm windows to put on
And salt and bird food by the ton

Someone who doesn't dress in layers
Preparing well to go somewhere
Whose footwear doesn't lace so much
Whose fingers keep the sense of touch

Without devices to move snow
What would garages have to show?
If snow's not piled both deep and wide
How else till spring lost items hide?

Now, I know Shakespeare wrote the line
For Richard, he of devious mind
Who envied Ed the royal life
With which we northerners are rife

So we stay north when it gets cold
(Two domiciles can get so old!)
And traveling very far each year
Costs cash and time – pain in the rear

Up north, we like our change of scene
In wonderland, first white then green
We balance outside with the in
Call it contentment or win-win

A WINTER DRIVE

The sky is snowing softly down
As we walk out the door
To drive the road to Canada
We know there will be more

But we northerners like the snow
It is a lovely day
Just five below, five hours to go
Adventure on the way

The chance to see a moose or deer
Ravens or eagles fly
Pink grosbeaks flocked upon the white
Some other nice surprise

The dusky road with icy strips
Curves gently through the woods
With front-wheel drive and snow-tires too
We go slow, as we should

The pines and firs on either side
Brush back the lowered sky
And frame our world of falling snow
As we glide slowly by

What better way to spend the day
(Though encapsulated)
Than watching nature's show outside
Beauty understated

Sharing it with your closest friend
The partner in your life
Riding beside you through the storm
Together man and wife

WATER SPRITES

Have you seen water sprites at play
O'er darkest deep beyond the bay?
Out where the white gulls seldom sail
Where crossing winds and waves prevail

One wintry day at clear high noon
I saw them dancing, heard no tune
Both up and down and back and forth
They number thousands here, up north

On the Big Lake their misty forms
Would make you think that it was warm
Though breezes blew, cold waves surged strong
The water sprites just played along

They rode the surges to and fro
Though shoreward far they did not go
I saw them on the wavelets' crests
Like human surfers at their best

Still farther out they looked like fog
Such "sea smoke" now just one big clog
No spritely motion, just a roll
Obscuring my view, on the whole

Perhaps sprites dance in coldest air
To keep as warm as their wet lairs
Or maybe they just love the sun
And dance their praises, every one

Entranced by that ethereal scene
Diaphanous as in a dream
I feel joy and alone I pray
I'll often see the sprites at play

GIFTS GIVEN

A foot of snow has filtered down
Most of it fallen overnight
It smooths the contours of the ground
And sparkles in the morning light

The green boughs bow unto the earth
In awe of so much higher power
That now somehow has given birth
To this new world in a few hours

The depth of snow on trees alone
(Both green and leafless stood the test)
Makes one alert for woody moans
Let's brush the branches, give them rest

Then seek the path where yesterday
We walked an old familiar trail
But all's different to searching gaze
Made level now, both hill and dale

Yet, there's something about what's fresh
Amidst a beauty new to you
That draws you on feeling your best
To value gifts, many or few

WINTER'S CHEER

The days grow short, the sun stays low
The skies fill softly now with snow
Gone are the autumn days of gold
The birds and flowers, colors bold

Yet winter brings its own sweet charm
With days so cold and nights so warm
By fireside light with friends so dear
When memory's embers draw us near

And dreams for later on seem clear
Near hearth and home in winter's cheer

CHICKADEE JAMBOREE

A couple dozen chickadees
Can be a most amazing sight
From underneath a bird feeder
In winter woods' cold evening light

Each comes to feed all on its own
From perch in aspen or in pine
Then grabs a seed, flies to a branch
To crack the hull, and that takes time

They have a choice to dine or hide
The seed for eating later on
In the long winter's icy grip
Or when their seed bonanza's gone

You hear their small wings everywhere
Claws on the feeders and the bark
Scolding when others come too close
With frenzied chirps – it's nearly dark

The tapping as they crack the seeds
Rings sharply in the clear night air
Percussion rhythms – chips and whirs
Such subtle sounds say birds are there

And if you look beneath the trees
You find seed hull piles on the ground
The evidence of forays made
Remains of seeds that small birds pound

I'd guess maybe three flocks are here
Each one is eight or ten birds strong
They seem so driven, organized
Maybe that's why they get along

WINTER CANVAS

Out on a run one snowy day
On newly whitened road
I left some large and frequent tracks
But I was not alone

It bothered me that where I trod
Disturbed the virgin snow
Tracks smaller and more delicate
Would have less chance to show

The red squirrel prints that I saw there
Were distinctive outlines
Larger back feet ahead of front
I crossed them many times

Some hurried, jumping in big bounds
Space between prints quite long
Others appeared to hop slowly
Their tracks wandering along

Deer tracks followed the snowy road
Some fairly large, some small
If they were made at the same time
The doe and fawns from fall

A gimpy buck not seen since spring
Has not left his dragged track
And though he's been around for years
I don't think he'll be back

Mouse prints left in the dark of night
Always look so confused
Crisscrossing themselves many times
Revisiting old news

There in the middle of the road
Then off the road, then back
A fox meandered in the dark
Leaving single-file tracks

Our suet was stolen earlier
A pine marten suspect
His bounding double prints now seen
Maybe the other sex

A ruffed grouse or one of her brood
Left tracks near our garage
Though off the road, her feathered load
On feet now winter-large

The snowshoe hare we sometimes see
Did not leave its large prints
I hope he munches cedar still
But so far there's no hint

I seldom view a wolf track here
They're usually on the lake
I wonder what prey he takes there
Do otters make mistakes?

My winter's canvas soon will fill
With tracks of car and plow
But it will often be renewed
Between next spring and now

NUTHATCHES

Whether the breast be white or red
These birds like standing on their heads
At first it may produce a frown
(We're not so used to upside-down)

And as nuthatches walk down trees
Small insect prey they often seize
They seem to find food storage nooks
That heads-up birds have overlooked

Perhaps these birds with weight up front
Use gravitation in the hunt
With small rear-ends up in the air
They stay face-down without a care

I've heard they're sometimes called "ass-ups"
The emphasis placed on their butts
But I like how they move so fast
Though I wish looks at them would last

At feeders, they're real "nutcases"
Snatch a seed, off to the races
They never seem relaxed or still
Perhaps they never eat their fill

Whatever you make of their name
In wintertime they seem quite tame
As they fill a most special niche
And leave bird watchers' lives enriched

HOAR FROST

Deciduous and evergreen
So powdered sugar bright
Whoever spread wonder around
Just came and went last night

From highest tree to shortest shrub
Each branchlet frosty now
The leafless woods awash with white
Bleak winter gone somehow

The ghostly pallor on the trees
Against the foggy skies
Brightens an otherwise gray day
A white-on-white disguise

And yet, with Christmas season nigh
There could be some red bows
To give the winter wrappings cheer
Contrast with fog and snow

BREAKING TRAIL

Snowshoe tracks there in the snow
Ordered offset patterns show
Meshed and tapered, two-by-two
Pointing both ways, ringing true

Leaving imprints on their way
Whether laid by night or day
With the snowshoes I have brought
I can follow them or not

Others' tracks that mark the trail
Show the way, ease my travail
Help me get there in less time
Save expenditure in kind

But I am not in a rush
There is no real need to push
Adventure is why I'm here
That and exercise, both dear

So I'll go where my heart leads
It's a compass I must heed
Often paths found on my own
Satisfy and lead to home

A HAWK OWL

A hawk owl tops an old gray snag
A tasty breakfast vole to bag
He hunts by day for all to see
On open land from wire or tree

His head is large, swiveled around
To peer at me without a sound
His eyes a piercing yellow stare
As if to ask, "Why are you there?"

His breast is barred, a spotted crown
His sideburns black, his eyes look down
He has a sort of facial disk
Catching soft sounds, lest they be missed

Suddenly – with a final stare
Alert to sound or movement there
He drops (to voles, not heaven-sent)
His long tail rudders his descent

A brief adjustment in the snow
And talons heavy, up he goes
To eat his catch on that same perch
A prelude to another search

THERE'S ALWAYS SOMETHING

The fir did not have far to fall
To bridge the gravel road
Its old dead branches weighted down
With snow – a heavy load

The windstorm snapped it eight feet up
And left an upright trunk
Five-foot-high snow banks stopped the drop
And in them it was sunk

Long brittle branches filled the road
And stuck out all around
The interweaving of the twigs
Obscured the snowy ground

We came upon the fallen fir
That dark and windy night
Our way home blocked by nature's ways
Surprise by bright car light

Headlights left on to check the scene
We found we could not lift
The tree out of its snowy grooves
Stuck firmly in the drifts

So, we dug down to where the fir
Was sunk in piled-up snow
And smoothed a path for it to slide
When rocked hard to and fro

With branches pruned and leveled snow
The way was cleared ahead
To swivel the tree off the road
And we drove home to bed

PERSISTENCE PAYS

One winter's day I chanced to see
A pine marten in a fir tree
As I sat working in my home
Both he and I were all alone

He sat and watched me watching him
In his sleek coat – brown with gray trim
Through a cold window we looked long
Mutual curiosity strong

But suet holders on nearby trees
Turned his bright eyes away from me
I saw that he had found a few
And now a new one was in view

From a rain gutter it hung down
I'm not quite sure martens can frown
But soon he moved right under it
And stared up at it for a bit

He tried a few jumps that fell shy
Then left, came back, gave it more tries
I thought I had him, mark my words
That suet would be just for birds

Again he left, results were nil
But in a half hour down the hill
He climbed a nice tall cedar tree
So suet feeder he could see

Then he descended, climbed again
Back up to where he once had been
I think the marten had just learned
How to get that for which he yearned

For soon I heard him on our roof
And what comes close to being proof
I saw the suet abruptly rise
Over the gutter toward the sky

It soon fell to the ground beneath
The marten followed, snow not deep
And gulping suet by the chunk
His look at me was pure "slam-dunk!"

ANGEL OF DEATH

I saw the downy hit the pane
Straight-on with sturdy bill
He crumpled down in a free-fall
There on our window sill

Woodpeckers often kill themselves
When they strike window glass
Despite their open-closed wing flight
They fly so hard and fast

But this one sat with his head raised
And moved it all around
I thought I'd give him time to heal
Then he'd be outward bound

But suddenly a shadow fell
With wings obscenely long
A northern shrike lit on the bird
With feet, though large, not strong

A razor bill delivered bites
They numbered only two
To downy's neck – and that was that
Nothing I could then do

A striking black and white killer
With convict stripes and mask
Caught in the act without remorse
Efficient to the task

With half-bent wings and open bill
The shrike gave me a stare
Like a hawk mantled over prey
As I rose from my chair

It turned and flew off down the slope
Downy in bill and claws
The prey weight half that of the shrike's
Was carried without pause

Predation is a natural act
Still, it is hard to take
You wish the outcome could be changed
For your and the prey's sake

WOLVES ON ICE

Three wolves came loping down the lake
One gray, one white, one black
Two in the lead spaced far apart
The third one farther back

They ran directly to their goal
Though each took different paths
The one that lagged ran with a limp
Its coat a bright coal black

Last night a deer killed on the ice
By wolves, these three, at least
Had been fed on before the light
Come back to keep the feast

The big gray wolf was the first there
He sat and looked around
Without his long legs under him
Just a lump on the ground

The white one arrived next, then stopped
And waited for a time
Then at some signal both arose
And you could say they dined

They pulled off pieces, chewed on bones
When it's fun, time just flies
I watched them through a spotting scope
The morning soon passed by

The black wolf arrived, ate its fill
As the first two lay near
No squabbles occurred when all fed
They showed no signs of fear

Eventually, the gray got up
And loped off at a trot
The other two wolves watched him go
But stayed in the same spot

The white soon followed to the west
They'd come down from the north
They both were very small before
The black one ventured forth

It trotted north, the way they'd come
A couple miles or more
And stayed out on the open ice
Bound for the farthest shore

On snowshoes then, we checked the kill
Some good meat still remained
But wolves finished that very night
What ravens had disdained

OWL TALK

Have you all heard the barred owl call?
"Who cooks for you, who cooks for y'all"
It rings out in bare winter woods
And often where you think it should

And sometimes from a nearby tree
You hear a wild cacophony
Of two owls yelling, taking turns
Or interrupting; how one yearns

To know their language, grasp their words
And understand why silent birds
Will sometimes fill the air with noise
Like children playing, girls and boys

Or does their chatter mean much more?
So scare a mouse, it ends in gore
Or woo a mate, or chew one out
In some extended scornful bout

An owl that can communicate
Most often when it's very late
Might not have much advice to give
But makes a better place to live

SKIING OUT

The snow lies soft o'er winter's ice
A moon-drenched lake invites me twice
To don my skis and live the cold
My cozy fire says "bad advice"

Still, Nature's song can be so strong
I can't resist it, not for long
And leaving comfort's grasp behind
Just feels so much more right than wrong

Soon striding, gliding in the night
Produces warmth 'neath God's cold light
As darkened cedars, spruce and pine
Provide a frame for ghostly white

A trail of wolf tracks in the snow
Gives me pause and chills as I slow
I think of deer on sharpened feet
Pursued and sliding, then brought low

And looking back for what's behind
I seek out trouble I don't find
When I should really be the wolf
Less chased than chaser, in my mind

Then turning back home down the lake
I follow tracks I had to make
To journey inward once again
For past, present and future's sake

SPRING

EARLY SPRING 1

Whitetails graze south-facing slopes
Winter now in patches there
Evergreens still clothed with white
Spring's warm sun will strip them bare

Lakes covered with slushy ice
Thick, save where cold water flows
Streams, still iced where current lags
Now their rippling beauty show

Clouds flower in open sky
Billowy forms of gray and white
Here and there a dark one blooms
Rain may fall on us tonight

If it does, it's to the good
Sooner then, the snow will go
So in concert with the sun
The symphony of life can flow

EARLY SPRING 2

A winter's worth of layered gray snow
Melts off our roof, but awfully slow
The gutters catch the frigid melt
Then cold returns and ice is held

Icicles glisten like wet tears
Produced by Winter, feeling fears
Of losing a long season's work
To her, warm sun a doubtful perk

But slowly, Spring's bright sun grows strong
Having its way as days grow long
Our home's warm white cap is now shed
Exchanged for naked roof instead

Man's active work then starts anew
I guess it's welcomed by a few
Cleaning chimneys, windows, shutters
Raking sticks, repairing gutters

And soon will come Spring's bright renewal
Birds, blooms, butterflies – nature's jewels
But gosh, the outside looks so drab
I miss the snow we used to have!

SPRING CLEANSING

The talk in town is about spring
And all the changes it will bring
The budding trees, greens from the ground
And outside-living all around

Snow on the melt, now mud and ice
The weather Minnesota-nice
The sun's rays strong upon your face
Soon cold will vanish from this place

Then Easter Day the snow arrives
The winter season is reprised
Some might call it resurrected
Not at all what was expected

Jack Frost stole back in overnight
And made the world seem clean and bright
But he knows winter's almost past
And to that thought we'll all hold fast

Yet, for a short time Easter Day
The world in pure white blankets lay
We'll just wait longer for the spring
Secure in hope that Easter brings

APRIL SNOW

The April sun is beating down
Upon the snow left on the ground
A spring snowstorm has dropped three feet
Then six more inches in a week

Snow still clings to balsam and pine
But more falls off with passing time
Springtime will win the yearly row
Winter's long reign ended for now

Within days, new grass will appear
And beckon to the hungry deer
Soon water from the melting snow
Will stimulate wildflowers to grow

And water from the deep snowpack
Will bring the lakes and rivers back
To levels not known here for years
Boat and canoe now without fear

Perhaps well-water might just last
Another year till summer's past
When visitors have come and gone
Rain water for garden and lawn

There's much that's good in April snow
Even when heavy; and we know
What is perhaps the nicest thing
It rapidly gives way to spring

THUNDER SNOW

The cold front had just passed on through
It was after midnight
Snow fell from the dark clouds above
The ground once brown now white

Another less-than-welcome storm
To set the season back
The temperature was twenty-nine
And wind we did not lack

As I sat in a darkened house
I heard a muffled sound
Lightning had flashed off to the west
Soft snow fell all around

The snow muffled both light and sound
Lightning, thunder muted
Storm distance, just about a mile
That is undisputed

Such winter storms are pretty rare
Just a few times a year
Mostly seen over the Great Lakes
Less so inland, like here

They say that it does happen, though
In large and mature storms
Fronts with moisture, move in high
Start currents if they're warm

More snow fell gently day and night
From this occluded storm
Birds were caught traveling north in spring
No one had thought to warn

They landed on the whitened roads
On frozen lakes, in woods
Blackbirds, juncos, thrushes, sparrows
Surviving where they could

I kept busy spreading out food
Over snow on the ground
Obliterated all too soon
Birds scratched for what they found

The snow depth, six inches or more
Not much for thunder snow
Sometimes five feet fall locally
I'm glad that wasn't so!

ICE-OUT TIME

The ice has pulled away from shore
The blanket doesn't fit the bed
The pock-marked surface, green and worn
A ragged comforter instead

The bay ducks feed – though just a few
The first to use the birthing lake
They dive the narrow rim of blue
Beneath the ice, make no mistake

The sheet can still hold eagle weight
Two stand far out like polar bears
Their white heads search, not for a mate
A vantage point for dinner fare

Two river otters glide and chase
They slip and slide in social play
Across the icy interface
Plunging for fish along the way

Two merlins twitter in the pines
The smaller mounts the larger's back
Their treetop flights form ties that bind
I guess it is the time for that

From leafless tangle, loud and long
A winter wren's song fills the air
Save robins' cheery morning song
The woods are winter-like and bare

Before long, whitethroats will appear
To add some music to the score
The loons, ospreys and gulls are here
They'll use the open water more

But early spring's a time to wait
For newness in each passing day
A time to watch, anticipate
As nature's quickening holds sway

CRANE SONG

How loud the rolling music sounds
Yet hangs so gently o'er the fields
The air reverberates around
To pipes within, the outside yields

The haunting sound of early spring
Of single bird or family flock
That through the dawning fresh air brings
To me, reminder to take stock

Of spring and time that flows along
Spent well in places free and wild
Where cold mist hangs with wild crane song
Suspended – a sound undefiled

Then sandhills, ghostlike, close to me!
Shapes now emerge in gathering light
Replacing aural symphony
And question whether sound trumps sight

WARBLER WALK

I know I have had better days
But today I was just amazed
The sun was bright, a gentle breeze
The birds were active in the trees

We had a couple hours to share
A walk with friends for whom we care
An easy trail through marsh and woods
Watching warblers, because we could

Wood warblers are a striking group
Males in bright-colored breeding suits
Flowers that move o'er sky and earth
It's little things that give life worth

Thirty-some species here in spring
Some stay to breed, summer joy bring
Some migrate farther to the north
We'll see them in the fall once more

Ovenbirds sing from low branches
With such loud songs, why take chances
These warblers nest upon the ground
They're quiet then, don't make much sound

Yellow warblers, bright in the sun
We had a super look at one
Red dashes stood out on his breast
He posed, knowing he was the best

We saw American redstarts
Startling bugs with flashing red parts
Their wings and tails opened and shut
Insects were scarce, there was no glut

Trim Nashville warbler with eye ring
We heard quite a few others sing
We didn't see his reddish crown
He kept his gray head feathers down

Common yellowthroat heard and seen
In sedge near water, he looked green
Then he turned and with yellow breast
And blackest mask, passed any test

And there, along the nearest shore
A northern waterthrush and more
He hunted shoreline, did his dance
Turned all around; we were entranced

A golden-winged warbler was close
Gold crown, shoulders; black cheeks and throat
He and female, rarer than some
Consensus best, when day was done

We saw more palm warblers, perhaps
Than other kinds, with rusty caps
Green on their backs, yellow below
On or near ground, tails on the go

Yellow-rumped warblers with white throats
Flycatching, giving short call notes
Yellow side spots; white on the brow
Active both high and low right now

Walking on branches, searching trees
Black-and-white warblers catching meals
Nuthatchy birds, more streaked than some
Hard to mistake, shadow or sun

Bright yellow on eyebrow and cheeks
Jet black throat – a black-throated green
And he will sing all summer long
His "Trees, trees, murmuring trees" song

White shoulder patches that stand out
Magnolia warblers leave no doubt
The male is a striking fellow
Throat, breast, belly brilliant yellow

A Wilson's warbler with black cap
Jauntily forward, not far back
Active in bushes, catching flies
Long tail and greenish, of small size

A Cape May warbler in one place
Chestnut cheeks on bright yellow face
White wing patches and yellow rear
We saw a male, but not his peers

Other birds we had hoped to view
Mourning, Blackburnian, to name two
We did not see – but what the heck
And nobody got "warbler neck"!

WILD ONE

We've seen his track on our small lake
Not quite as big as some wolves make
But still respectable in size
A presence that we came to prize

For nine years we have called this home
And always his tracks have been close
Together with his hairy scat
Deer sense him too, I'd bet on that

There is a wolf pack, or has been
Some say nine members, maybe ten
But we have seldom heard them howl
Nor seen them running cheek to jowl

One evening as I used the phone
A gray wolf loped by me alone
Across the yard from left to right
Mottled pelage, not black or white

Time slowed as the wolf passed me by
I saw the fire in yellow eye
Big feet, full tail and long gray legs
His focus steady, straight ahead

Whatever he could see or smell
Maybe a deer, I couldn't tell
He didn't see me standing there
Chill up my back with raised neck-hair

Transfixed alone in time and space
Struck dumb by wolfish power and grace
I was again a naïve child
Caught in the spirit of what is wild

FOX NEWS

She travels muddy township roads
Part of her nightly rounds
Her delicate tracks in a line
Between her hunting grounds

We don't see her come every night
Nor do our lakeside friends
But she uses our land and theirs
As a means to her ends

She leaves some perfume from night hunts
It hangs in daylight air
We often know in morning's light
That she has just been there

A vixen red fox in her prime
With sharp and lively face
Black stockings set off slender legs
She holds her tail with grace

She often hunts near our garage
For mice that shelter there
How successful she is, who knows
We have some mice to spare

Each winter we have fat ruffed grouse
That roost beneath the snow
By spring, I bet the fox finds one
Fewer grouse then, I know

I've seen her pounce in meadow grass
Her front feet in the air
A lovely dance, there is a chance
A vole is dinner fare

I guess she put us on her route
Because we feed the birds
As do the other neighbors near
At least that's what I've heard

In winter she eats our bird seeds
Or suet on the ground
The manners of our feeder birds
Are not the best around

One time outside, with suet in hand
I whistled just to see
If she'd come closer like a dog
Or run away from me

She looked intently at my hand
Then slowly walked my way
I dropped the suet, she snapped it up
She scarcely let it lay

She's raised pups in a gravel pit
Less than a mile away
The land is subdivided now
They'll build on it some day

Maybe she'll keep us in her world
Or will one of her pups
Until we're gone, more people come
Or "progress" catches up

KAYAKING

She turns her torso to the left
Pulls left blade back along her side
As right arm pushes right blade out
To flash in sunlight, wide and high

Then torso right as blade dips in
The front blade pushed out once again
As knees against the cockpit hold
Her legs stretched forward down within

Her rudder pedals help her brace
Against the shifting, side to side
That paddling with two blades can bring
And serve to give a truer ride

Low to the water as she goes
And quiet with a gentle glide
She views floating and shoreline life
As she enjoys a springtime ride

Cedars browsed by winter's deer
Create a high and even line
The yellow pollen from pine trees
Floats on lake surface, scattered fine

A few beds of marsh marigolds
Bright yellow in their narrow strands
Their lively color brightens up
The wash between the lake and land

Whirligig beetles spin around
In groups on the lake's surface cold
A few mayflies have also hatched
And black flies too, if truth be told

There near the shore, two wood ducks leap
Straight up from where they tipped for food
They could have stayed, the kayak turned
Their sudden movement breaks the mood

A kingfisher, newly returned
Rattles his greeting to her craft
His fishing stopped for a short time
He switches perches, then looks back

The ospreys have not used their nest
Though they are fishing down the shore
She wonders as she glides beneath
And watches a bald eagle soar

Two loons surface, close to her bow
One touches base with a low "hoot"
They separate from her and now
Tremolo calls, liquid and loose

A peaceful time on a small lake
Lost in the outside world she loves
Relaxed now, she takes a short break
The kayak still and nothing moves

A motor boat roars down the lake
It's not too long till opening day
Her kayak rocks some in its wake
She waits   and soon waves fade away

AIR SHOW

Cherry-red bills pointed straight down
Caspian terns, small fish now found
After searching the lake below
They fold wings, plunge in – quite a show

Smaller bodies, much smaller bills
Common terns too, will catch their fill
Some sit on buoys, tails tilted high
Resting from hunts in windy sky

Noisy gulls fly high overhead
I wish they'd go elsewhere instead
Mostly, they are the ring-billed kind
Herring, Franklin's we also find

Pelicans fly a conga line
Half of the flock slowly unwinds
To splash down in shallows below
The others have someplace to go

Canada geese are flying in pairs
Like mid-range bombers in the air
Returning from the stubble fields
Full of good roughage from their meals

Mallard ducks trade forth, and then back
And usually with their anxious quacks
Lone males seem always on the go
Looking for love both high and low

Loons often give their crazy calls
As one, two, three fly over all
But if too high, they may sneak by
Watch for their humped backs in the sky

Tree swallows swooping – looks like fun
Blue and white birds flash in bright sun
Here and there is a tail that forks
Do barn swallows achieve more torque?

Broad-winged hawks fly over the shore
Frogs and small snakes there to hunt for
Tails with broad bands of black and white
Short wings, black "fingertips" in flight

Two ospreys with their talons clasped
Fall together, hit with a splash
On their backs they come undone
Two birds no longer joined as one

Grebes and rails in the undercroft
They're hardly ever seen aloft
In autumn, they'll fly to the coast
But now they walk or dive or float

Just a couple hours near a lake
Though it's a big one, give or take
With binocs and a comfy seat
A spring air show is hard to beat

A NORTHERN MARSH

I love a northern marsh in spring
Cattails frazzled with winter wear
Bulrushes, sedges also bring
No sign of life or warming there

Giant phragmites reeds stand in clones
Stalks and wispy heads still remain
Despite a winter's heavy snows
Their eight- to twelve-foot height retained

Nearby, grain stubble fields from fall
And other plants with fruit and seed
Provide food for those large and small
But soon new growth will meet that need

Muskrats and beavers here and there
Paddle in stream and pond and lake
Their houses, still their springtime lairs
Lookouts for geese and eagles make

Ospreys and eagles in the air
Courting and hunting in the marsh
Nest high on platforms, dead trees there
Exposed to weather, mild or harsh

Northern harriers hunt marsh borders
Gray males, brown females, white rumps show
Cruising low, their patrols ordered
They catch small rodents down below

Painted turtles now on the move
Females looking for nesting sites
Males move to summer places too
Where they wintered is now not right

Frog song is heard both day and night
Peepers, chorus frogs, others mate
Their calls may slow when day is bright
But breeding season cannot wait

Brown bitterns wheel in cloudy sky
Their heron shapes easy to spot
It's good to see a bird so "shy"
Camouflaged "freezing" more their lot

Blue herons hunt marshes every day
In flight, their long necks folded in
They search the shallows for their prey
Amphibians or those with fins

Male snipe courtship now skyward-sent
As birds rise and fall in the air
Their tail feathers whistle on descent
Hard-to-place "winnows" here and there

Other shorebirds coming, leaving
Snipe and spotted sandpipers stay
Killdeer remain, their cries grieving
Those now departing on their way

Coots float in numbers near the shore
White frontal shields shine in the sun
Where you see one, you will see more
Feet pattering on takeoff runs

Diving ducks gather in large rafts
Riding out strong waves and high winds
Restless, they abandon their crafts
As their flights north begin again

Scores of tree swallows, just come north
Struggling against the strong wind's surge
They make slight progress in the force
Nor will bugs sought, when they emerge

Male redwings have chosen prime spots
To flash red wings, sing "konk-a-ree"
To striped females who, like as not
Will soon arrive, start families

White swans float – graceful long necks high
Or feed forever, necks submerged
It seems they're no longer alive
Then heads pop up, each with a lurch

Sandhill cranes, still in family groups
Their gray plumage brownish with clay
Bugling calls announce spring anew
I watch them feed and fly and play

Cranes have a most deliberate walk:
Three toes lifted to dangle down
Graceful slow steps where'er they stalk
Each foot forward, just clearing ground

Canada geese on islands, banks
Strong defenders of their nest sites
Against trespassers they close ranks
They're always ready for a fight

Grouped horned grebes, seven in number
Now sleep with golden "horns" that touch
Covey-like, organized slumber
Yet set to dive, gone in a rush

Sedge wrens, though there appears a lack
Of evidence for a good place
Have chosen their coldwater flats
Where they'll perpetuate the race

Gray-faced swamp sparrows sing slow trills
Yellowthroats flash bright, when in view
Both choose the marsh, stay there until
Nestlings have fledged, feathers are new

Some songbirds stop, replenish stores
Of fat, and rest for a few days
No one is really keeping score
But when abundant, they're called "waves"

In spring the marsh is less at peace
More fun with movement and new mates
Too soon migration, action cease
Abundance, new growth dominate

I think what makes a spring marsh cool
Is its many and diverse forms
Some living there, some passing through
As spring's new life and weather warm

COUNTING COOS

He counted coos along the way
They were the gentle kind
He didn't have to take a scalp
Hit someone from behind

He counted them on small town streets
And farmland far and wide
Out on the plains, in scrub and brush
Throughout the countryside

In springtime, all across the land
Others were counting too
For mourning doves call then, you know
At least the male birds do

To attract mates and form pair bonds
Keep other males away
Renew the ancient song and dance
That keeps their kind in play

And in the fall, hunt doves or not
Isn't it nice to know
That someone's watching out to see
If numbers fall or grow?

Would it were so for all the gifts
That nature gives to us
We often wait till things are gone
Then raise an awful fuss

Like frogs in water on a stove
Brought slowly to high heat
We realize our problems when
They're hardest to defeat

LOST AND FOUND AND LOST

He knew just what it had to be
As they drove by the lifeless form
He shouted "Stop!" They backed to see
How much the carcass had been harmed

And as he held it gently there
All but unmarked, it seemed a shame
This graceful creature of the air
Was now no more, with car to blame

He'd watched such birds from earth and air
In Florida's vast grassy marsh
Their range constrained, their presence rare
Protected in our nation's park

It was a dead swallow-tailed kite
Once seen in Minnesota skies
A striking sight in black and white
In death, as in life, to be prized

Kites once built nests in our tall trees
But they lay just two eggs per nest
Late in the nineteenth century
Their flights became a gunner's test

Like big barn swallows they once swooped
Low over swampland, prairies, bogs
Hunting their prey, sometimes as groups
Mostly insects, small snakes and frogs

Kites do 'most all things as they fly
They court on high and form pair bonds
They eat their prey while they soar by
And bathe by skimming lakes and ponds

They even nest high in the air
In tall pines, cypress or hardwoods
Nests lined with old man's beard up here
Or southern Spanish moss – both good

Kites no longer breed in our state
But some wander to their old range
Our southern swamps now hold their fate
There are some things we just can't change

SUMMER

SITTING ON THE DOCK

Upon a summer's afternoon
As day draws to a close
On cedar bench on cedar dock
We sense what comes and goes

Mosquitoes have not found us yet
We're out over the lake
Some dragonflies land at our feet
Small hunters need a break

Out on the point a waterthrush
Sings loud and cheerful songs
As he explores the water's edge
And branches all along

A red squirrel scolds us from the shore
Our low talk he must hear
Or does he see slight movements as
We sip on our cold beer?

A ring-billed gull near the far shore
Flies slowly, loosely on
Its white shape moving gracefully
Too soon the moment's gone

A beaver swims close, head held high
The rest of him submerged
He looks at us with baleful eye
We have a lethal urge

For years we have enjoyed his kind
But then he dropped a birch
Across our dock – 'twas more than rude
For us it was a first

The rattle of a kingfisher
Near us but out of sight
We watch for it and finally see
Her breast band in low light

Two loons now round the island point
No youngsters swim along
They do not fish, they slowly glide
One sings a loonly song

A nesting platform has been placed
On our island's far side
We'll see if they tried nesting there
On our next kayak ride

A motor boat comes into view
Two neighbors wave hello
They're off to catch a fish or two
Before the sunset's glow

Through binocs we both watch them go
They fade away from view
We spot two turtles on a log
Perhaps they're watching too

As day gives way to twilight time
We start to feel the chill
Though we love sitting on the dock
We head back up the hill

SUMMERTIME VACATIONS

At most we had a week or so
For our vacations at the lake
It never seemed quite long enough
So much to do, to contemplate

We traveled from the place we lived
Through all the towns along the way
We kids would almost give up hope
It must have taken half a day

On weekends there we had to share
The cabin with cousins who'd come
From far and wide, where they all lived
Although I guess I did like some

For others there was a long dock
To cannonball them as they swam
Or beaches for them to help clean
So weeds would not clog up the sand

We played good games with cards and boards
Had diving contests with them too
Some kids were smart and some athletic
Some things we did then were brand new

Up at the lake we fished the dock
With red-white bobbers and cane poles
We put the worms we dug on hooks
And touched the water with our toes

We rowed ourselves with heavy oars
To Grandpa's diving dock on floats
Where perch and sunfish found some shade
We fished out there with tied-up boat

Sometimes, of course, we swam and dove
And rested under the dock's shade
Or watched the fish through snorkel masks
Touched bottom on the dives we made

My dad sometimes let me go out
In the canoe all by myself
To cast for bass along the weeds
Or off the point on rocky shelf

We got to shoot our BB guns
Ride Grandpa's horses to the barn
Sleep at night on a big screen porch
Hear insects humming without harm

We used the outhouse in the woods
Helped clean it and the trails around
Swung in the hammock out in front
And listened to the outdoor sounds

What blessings our vacations held
At Grandpa's cabin on the lake
The treasured times we spent as kids
On our summer vacation breaks

CHILDHOOD BOAT RIDES

On perfect Sunday afternoons
My grandpa set the travel course
For a boat ride around the lake
The outboard – just a seven horse

We all thought Grandpa's boat was great
It carried seven folks or more
All crowded close on wooden seats
Sometimes a dog sat on the floor

We'd go out for about two hours
Often the wind and waves washed in
Bow-riders could get soaking wet
When we quartered too thick or thin

We imagined from whom we passed
The lives of adults and their kids
Where they were from, what they were like
Where they had been, just what they did

We checked up on neighbors and friends
Inspected docks, boats, and lake yards
Most people waved as we went by
On Sundays they weren't working hard

We watched gulls fly, both young and old
Looked out for loons and their small chicks
Hoped for bald eagles and ospreys
We all enjoyed their aerial tricks

We passed by some good weedy beds
Including those we had fished last
Saw other spots that we could try
And where Dad once caught a big bass

The ladies also got ideas
On how best to improve a place
With flowers, trees or furniture
Attractive yards were no disgrace

We brought cold drinks, maybe a snack
To last until the ride was done
And our binocs helped us to see
On family boat rides, just for fun

CASTING LOTS

Some good things come to those who bait
But I'd rather cast out than wait
A big fish might just hit my lure
Nothing in life is ever sure

It's really more of a big mess
To use live bait, and I confess
That impaling small living things
To me, thoughts of Dracula brings

And critters brought from near and far
Released in our lakes might just mar
What for a long time has evolved
Create more problems to be solved

Dad's tackle box provided cures
For empty stringers; full of lures
For northerns, muskies, bass, walleyes
His kids fish like him, no surprise

So though I drown worms with grandkids
Jig minnows too on different rigs
I prefer casting plug or spoon
It gives the feel of elbow room

Besides, my tackle box looks neat
When opened wide there at my feet
The lures arranged neatly in rows
Some useful, others just for show

Mepp's spinners in several sizes
Metal minnows in disguises
Some dardevles, striped red and white
To catch the big ones day and night

River runts, other deep runners
Find the fish not where the sun is
Shad raps that dive to different depths
Search out the small and large fish left

Bucktails, black or brown with spinners
And rapalas, often winners
Pikey minnows, bass-o-renos
Floating frogs to fish the weeds close

KB spoons, with their red glass eyes
Nip-a-dee-dees that some bass prize
Lures rattling, splashing, made for noise
Some catch fisherfolk seeking toys

Beyond the fake bait that you use
It's where you throw, how long you choose
To let it sink, and your retrieve
Think like a fish, make them believe

One muskie caught ten thousand casts
Not quite that bad for largemouth bass
Walleyes take artificials too
Though more take live bait than take spoons

And northern pike strike at your lures
I like to catch them, that's for sure
Walleyes taste better, that is true
But northerns grow big, fight well too

Now, mostly it's catch and release
Of fish and tensions so they'll cease
And each cast gives me one more chance
To contemplate life's happenstance

NIGHTHAWKS

Nighthawks traverse the darkened sky
At dawn and dusk you see them fly
Long of wing they swoop, glide and sweep
Their open mouths net insect feasts

You spot them in the gloomy light
And know it's nighthawks in full flight
High in the air, their feathered hands
Betrayed by wide, white wingtip bands

But even better in pitch black
They vocalize their air attacks
A nasal "peent" like a woodcock
Next to your head can be a shock

And courting males make "sonic booms"
Produced by wings as down they zoom
The females must find that a treat
Their flyboys have a cool wing beat

More likely though, in the night air
Around lampposts or anywhere
You'll see or hear these great night birds
They're cousins of the owls, I've heard

FISH HAWKS

On long bent wings with blackened wrists
He gives our ice-bound lake a look
It's good to add him to our list
Back from the seaside break he took

He hunts a dozen miles away
On open water for his meals
His mate arrives in a few days
When our lake's water is revealed

The pair takes turns hunting our pond
They hover, plunge and rarely miss
From two perches of which they're fond
They dry out and eat fresh-caught fish

They always carry prey they've caught
Fish head-end forward through the air
Probably not something that they're taught
But it gives them a certain flair

The great nest that they've used for years
They now repair for summer use
Built on an island, but we fear
This time it's had too much abuse

But the pair sticks, mates and lays eggs
They incubate about six weeks
The male hunts and when his mate begs
He feeds her – perhaps to stop shrieks

Two nestlings soon fill up the nest
It takes two months until they fly
Their parents then can get some rest
Start moving south, say their goodbyes

The eagles that harass our birds
Remain until the freeze-up comes
But ospreys that eat just live fish
Must look elsewhere for food and fun

So while the eagles eat dead meat
And scavenge for their wherewithal
The ospreys enjoy seafood treats
All winter and the rest of fall

RESCUE

A checkered black and white motif
Against the emerald grass
Glossy black neck and blood-red eye
A surreal mood is cast

Darkness approached as we drew near
The loon appeared intact
Wings tight to sides, he seemed aware
We looked and he looked back

A water bird beside dry road
Perhaps he hit a wire?
Now stranded far from watery home
Both out of place and tired

As we came close, he turned around
Our threat faced, after all
Surprise! He yodeled from the ground
A territorial call

Without a liquid runway, he
Was vulnerable to us
With legs far back on heavy frame
He managed awkward thrusts

We threw a blanket over him
Secured body and neck
Stuffed him in a large plastic tub
And tried not to get pecked

A short exam of wings and feet
Revealed no injuries
We found a placid nearby lake
A place for his release

"Our" swimming loon yodeled again
Did "wing flaps" several times
Three other loons swam in, maybe
To see displays so fine

The loon then dove, his feet worked well
But we will never know
If he belonged there on that lake
Or if he soon would go

BOBOLINKS AND MEADOWLARKS

The bobolinks have just arrived
Dull meadowlands have come alive
With songs that frolic through the air
As summer songsters sing them there

Though they nest down in grassy depths
The males have for the air, earth left
To court their females from on high
With frequent forays through the sky

A large hay field with power line
Old fence dividing yours and mine
Is not disdained by bobolinks
The prairie now a missing link

They take off with a burst of song
Ground-to-air ratio is not long
See them display, light shades above
Black underneath, not all for love

They've come in from the Argentine
So far to fly for family dreams
Bird airline meals are grass and rice
Summer pampas must still be nice

Just down the road in a low place
Some redwings breed and sometimes trade
Back and forth for a tasty bite
As cousins, I guess they have rights

Brewer's blackbirds (males have white eyes
Females have brown, and lack male size)
Build nests in grassy fields and trees
But don't need prairie, if you please

But meadowlarks prefer the grass
Their loud whistles bring joy that lasts
As they sing from both fence and ground
Their voices echo all around

Larks blend in with their tan, striped backs
But when they turn, drab aspect past
Bright yellow breasts, black v-shaped scarfs
And pudgy shapes say life's a lark

They fly low with their stiff-winged glides
And tails show white on either side
Lark wings and tails are broad and short
But serve quite well to bring birds north

Though prairie lands were once widespread
Now agriculture rules instead
Yet, grassland birds may still survive
Man's land use change and pesticides

THE TURKEY VULTURE

The turkey vulture soars on high
On cambered wing in blue clear sky
Its wings two-toned, its tiny head
So small it's hard to tell it's red

Much less to see it's featherless
For what it eats would make a mess
It lives on rotten meat, you know
And somehow smells it down below

And you can bet when it finds some
More turkey vultures soon will come
To gorge themselves on some dead thing
The end to which a car did bring

But scavenging has merit to it
Even our bald eagles do it
And what befits our national bird
Should not be criticized, I've heard

So let's not stoop to put on airs
And simplify from our soft chairs
What we demean, both near and far
May clean up something we have marred

ORIOLE OBLATION

A northern oriole is out back
His color and his voice both bold
Resplendent in bright orange and black
Loud whistled notes and rattling scold

He is a blackbird, after all
We're lucky his song's a step up
For you'd expect a harsher call
Like rusty gate opened or shut

And he adapts nicely to man
Though he pays what the small price is
He'll take what's given, when he can
Sugared water or orange slices

I like the way he scolds and sings
Sharing himself for human gifts
Wary of what good fortune brings
Yet grateful for what someone's left

Much like some prophets used to do
Cursing dependence on their god
And the hard rules to which they hewed
While blessing him, both staff and rod

MOSQUITO WAR

The summer started wet and still
With standing water everywhere
Undergrowth grew until it filled
The land with green – not much left bare

Mosquito larvae soon emerged
Adults took wing and even swarmed
Much like a military surge
They overwhelmed us and did harm

Aggressive females led the charge
First large and slow, then small and fast
They left lumps on our necks and arms
Their poison made the itching last

They penetrated Skin-So-Soft
And some got through a layer of DEET
Our defenses all done for naught
We strategized upon retreat

Both sides used chemicals, it's true
We stooped to citronella, Raid
We cut the grass and whacked weeds too
And their superior forces paid

But truth be told, they changed our lives
We slathered up, avoided woods
And when night fell we stayed inside
Fear and resentment were our moods

But on we went with tender skins
Homeland invaded, who would win?
We hoped that such terrorism
Would not cloud our future vision

For we knew life had to go on
We had to work, kayak and shop
Essentials life is based upon
Whether we're threatened or we're not

DANDELIONS

I respect the dandelion
More in your yard than in mine
It will grow well anywhere
Give it soil, water and air

Its scalloped leaves hug the ground
One long root to hold it down
You can dig up single plants
Deal with many, if you want

Salads, dandelion wine too
Come from leaves, leaves you can brew
And you're bound to have enough
Finding this plant is not tough

Van Gogh painted his sunflowers
But dandelions too, have power
To rouse you from verdant dreams
Their flowers bring you brighter themes

Silky seeds are arty too
Blown by wind puffs or by you
Drifting light on summer breeze
Floating down just where they please

Rub the blooms on a kid's face
An artistic change of pace
One you see and smell and feel
Face-art has its own appeal

Or weave yourself a 'lion chain
To chase sadness or some pain
Maybe give one to a friend
She may weave a brighter end

Even though we may not need
This small yellow common weed
I'm happy it is around
Cheering us when we are down

TINY TRAMPOLINES

A cool and misty summer morn
Bunchberry in full bloom
Mosquitoes crowd my walking path
I wish I had more room

A hermit thrush sings haunting songs
From somewhere in the woods
Bright lupine blooms beside the path
It's living where it should

But what really catches my eye
With dew still on the plants
Is tiny trampolines widespread
On grass and fern and branch

And even on herbaceous weeds
The small silk pockets shine
Some horizontal, but some not
Spiders don't seem to mind

The webs are not as beautiful
As garden spiders make
They're like the cobwebs in a house
But with a concave grace

The weavers use the finest silk
And modify web shape
To fit plants that they build upon
The ones they choose to drape

Small architects sit by their webs
And wait for insect prey
Then bounce out, grab and wrap it up
To eat another day

These tiny brownish animals
Are very hard to see
But webs reveal just where they are
To passersby like me

A JULY BICYCLE RIDE

Somewhere between too slow and fast
July biking can be a blast
You pedal fast to lose deer flies
But slow for plants and butterflies

Rusty pine needles on the ground
Make a subtle and swishing sound
As you ride over piles windrowed
And sometimes you can't miss pine cones

Monarchs fly near host milkweed plants
Wood nymphs spin in a circle dance
Bright swallowtails passed one by one
On lazy flights in shade and sun

Different sizes of dragonflies
Present a challenge for the eyes
They seem at peak abundance now
Mosquito-catchers – they know how

Baby crows croak from the tall trees
Oriole nests rock in summer breeze
Veerys sing their cascading songs
And call "vee-ear" all the day long

Tangled swamp roses you might pass
All run together, first to last
Columbines and lady slippers
Both showy – habitat differs

Least flycatchers repeat "chebec"
They're hard to spot on a bike trek
And yellowthroats and chickadees
Sing anytime the moments seize

Nearby hayfields have now been mowed
First cuttings are all neatly rowed
I hope that the ground-nesting birds
Have missed the cut, can still be heard

Wild daisy and dandelion fields
Brighten landscapes but have no yield
Of any economic kind
Yet fill the eye and soothe the mind

Indian paintbrush of orange-red
Two-toned yellow butter-and-eggs
Cotton grass, hazel, alder too
These and much more float into view

Silk globes of goat's beard here and there
Seed heads now ripe to ride the air
Three-inch "blow-balls" beside the road
Like dandelions with steroid loads

If you sit on a nice soft seat
Bike-riding can be a fine treat
You see more ground than on a walk
Meet more new people, stop and talk

So pedal slow, fast or just coast
Make stops, so you'll see some things close
Another way to be outside
Get into life, enjoy the ride!

A LAKEWALK RUN

The fog hung low on the big lake
As he began his morning run
He heard, not saw, the road above
As pale dawn gave way to the sun

The lakewalk path stretched out ahead
It cut a clean way through the fog
The lake was somewhere down below
He glimpsed some large rocks as he jogged

The fresh moist air filled up his lungs
Deep breathing cycles in the cold
His footfalls sounded on the ground
As counter-rhythm there took hold

Goldenrod, lupine, Queen Anne's lace
Floated by slowly as he went
Pink roses filled a small rosebush
He tried, but could not catch their scent

A robin fast-walked on the grass
(Like his own pace, he briefly thought)
It stopped in mid-path, searched for worms
The asphalt hunt would come to naught

Though berry clusters had not filled,
Some sumac leaves to orange had turned
A planted circle near wood bench
Day lilies, blue phlox and some ferns

White and gray gulls already soared
Young and old, their cries filled the air
A chipmunk scurried on its way
Risking exposure, but aware

He passed some walkers – ones and twos
Silent or chatty as they moved
Bicycles, runners, some unplugged
Some glassy-eyed, lost in their tunes

A song sparrow's bright familiar song
Was music to him as he ran
He saw the bird then, on a bush
Drifting by him, catch as catch can

The foghorn sounded from the point
He'd seen the schedule: lakers due
The fog was slowly lifting now
The Aerial Bridge not yet in view

His goal had not been beaucoup miles
But to raise metabolism
Turning around, he headed home
His wife and heart-rate long since risen

He reached and climbed the four switchbacks
Up to the level of the street
Now relaxed, wet with salty sweat
He knew an active life is sweet

RAIN

If there are forty words for snow
In Aleut or Eskimo
There should be even more for rain
For it is never quite the same

Eliza's "mainly on the plain"
Soaks grass and earth, here or in Spain
There isn't much to intercept
Or stop the fall to soil bereft

And wet stuff soaks in good earth too
Through thick organic layers, it's true
And percolates to deepest roots
So grasses can grow tender shoots

The rain that falls on desert plants
So starved for moisture and the chance
To flower, that they straightaway
Put forth their beauty within days

And insects, toads, and other forms
Quickened by rain, their rites perform
Awakened dormant desert life
Added to flowers late made rife

While in a rain forest with layers
Of vegetation, droplets fare
Much differently, some stopped or slowed
By epiphytes, trees, ferns that grow

If you but stand in such a place
You might not feel rain on your face
And quite enjoy the gentle sound
Of water slowly trickling down

With wind, rain can be something else
A driving force that really pelts
What's in its path can be knocked down
Leaves, branches, shingles, to the ground

And what of cold rains in the fall
That shouldn't be called rain at all
So cold they chill you to the bone
You can't wait to warm up at home

Cool summer rains can refresh you
Chase stagnant air, a blessing true
And the smell after such fine rains
Can make life seem renewed again

Summer rains can bring light and sound
Thunder and lightning all around
You may enjoy a great wet show
Though it's still good to see them go

Morning rain may come gently down
As you awaken, hear the sound
In tent or bed, an aural treat
Like pattering of little feet

Some rain you barely sense with skin
As mist-like it comes down and in
You can stand in it wearing clothes
And stay quite dry from head to toes

Rain that falls on a metal roof
Sounds joyously, far from aloof
The tempo may be fast or slow
It pitter-patters loud or low

And what about the acid kind
Tainted by factories or mines
It harms the life in streams and lakes
By driving down higher pH

Then there's the rain that puts out fires
Brings us cool drinks or makes lakes higher
Brings us hydroelectric power
Or may allow a longer shower

Rain comes down in different amounts
It floods, puddles, or doesn't count
Precipitation – as a "trace"
Or enough to make torrents race

Sometimes rainfall can last for days
And people start to look half-crazed
What's happening doesn't seem quite fair
It must be raining everywhere!

Why are some raindrops large and wet?
When they hit ground they need a net
While others melt into the earth
And gently give to new life, birth

It seems to me, when rain comes down
Nature is blurred in humid gown
As with the sunshine and the snow
It's one more gift to help us grow

HIGH SUMMER

They are so surreal on TV
In ads, those bright blue skies you see
With snow-white clouds piled up so high
They seem like stair-steps through the sky

And bushes, trees, and even grass
Cover the ground in greenish cast
The tones so varied that it seems
It's really not hard to be green

But real is better, just go forth
And live high summer in the north
The sun beats down, the angle's right
The days are long, not so the nights

Ambience sated, the air full
One can feel lazy, even dull
Summer's abundance starts to show
Crops in a field, fawns with a doe

July up north just stands alone
Soak up the feeling – take some home
To last you through the wintertime
For warmth and plenty soon decline

TWO ALONE

Wild rice leaves float in long green lines
Conforming with the wind and waves
As clear shallows they now define
Their presence dominates the bay

Some channel markers show one way
To avoid rice and escape out
But larger craft will there hold sway
We look for quiet water south

Our canoe skims across the plants
We break a few stems as we go
Once in a while we get the chance
To paddle where rice does not grow

Dragonflies hunt from broken stalks
Their glistening wings fill summer air
Biting flies in our canoe walk
To either end where legs are bare

A painted turtle can be seen
In clear water amidst the rice
Her carapace of darkest green
She slowly swims, surfaces twice

Mergansers appear near the shore
In single file, just a few birds
Then we catch sight of a few more
They skitter as we're seen and heard

Abruptly, a heron takes flight
Disturbed, it flies just fifty feet
Then drops back in, just out of sight
A common pattern, still a treat

In yellow kayak, a young boy
Comes out to greet us from his place
Proud of his skills in floating toy
He paddles with us at slow pace

He says his boat is "Benjamin"
There lettered by hand on the side
Then turns toward shore with a big grin
His dad gave Ben the boat to ride

We reach the point in the next bay
Where we must turn and head for home
We've spent some time on a fine day
Traveling together, yet alone

LAKE BREAK

Every time I see a lake
I always feel refreshed
By aqua incognito
(Like terra, but it's wet)

Sometimes I could jump right in
A cooling interlude
The thought alone renewing
Or maybe it's the mood

Often the water is deep
The bottom can't be seen
Plants and animals down there
Dark, slimy, fast and green

I could dive in just to see
What goes on down below
After which maybe I might
Know more than I did know

Cleansing one inside and out
Swimming's sacramental
Thought and action both refresh
It's so elemental

THE PORTAGE

Two paddles stem the Old Town's glide
And guide her gently into shore
The bowman steps over the side
Her feet on liquid land once more

He of the stern wets his two feet
Unloads Duluth packs, one by one
Till on dry land, bow and stern meet
The portage work has just begun

He helps her don the heavy pack
She takes the paddles and odd gear
And starts to trudge, with no look back
Focused on rocks and roots now near

He steps back in the sparkling lake
Lifts the canoe to waiting knee
Then flips her up without a scrape
Till carry-pads and shoulders meet

Carefully then, he walks ashore
Starts up the hill that faces him
Slowly for now, there's so much more
Hill crest ahead is but a rim

He knows he has to watch his boots
Be sure of foot on the sharp rocks
Not step on rounded, slippery roots
Be alert for canoe road-blocks

He sees wild flowers, for a while
Looks for the scats of moose and bear
Remembers when he's found their piles
Hopes he will not meet either here

The food pack's on the lake behind
There's no word of panhandling bears
But wilderness can be unkind
At least to people traveling there

More than a hundred rods to go
Each somewhat less than a canoe
And he's portaged enough to know
He'd like to rest before he's through

Maybe he'll find a half-downed tree
Or large rock somewhere on the way
To set his aching shoulders free
But he will make it, come what may

His thoughts return to here and now
He's reached a long and muddy swamp
He probes for firm footing somehow
Sinks often in the mud and damp

Finally, downhill to the new lake
Welcome, but almost worse than climb
The downward tilt of boat can make
Him lose his balance, break a limb

He picks a route to a good place
To set the boat in without harm
He wades in, flips her into space
Still attached by hand and arm

One trip back for the other packs
Trudge to the unknown shore again
Then both relax, as they look back
Just one last view of where they've been

Now ready for what lies ahead
They both feel a small sense of pride
What was uncertain, even dread
Has revealed yet a different side

AUTUMN

BOOTS

I first saw Boots, a whitetail buck
A full eight autumns back
He had white stockings on four feet
Like old high-button spats

His antlers displayed eight nice points
He was a good-sized deer
We put out corn in feeders then
And he would come quite near

He shed an antler on one side
I found it, picked it up
A quite substantial piece of bone
I kept it for good luck

Then one November come the hunt
Boots took a shoulder shot
Two hunters tracked him from afar
His bloody trail ran hot

He limped across our frozen lake
To an island offshore
They followed him back to our land
Where he lay down was gore

We let the hunters search the place
We thought the buck would die
But they could never find old Boots
Though they made a good try

We saw him after season's end
His left front leg hung limp
All through the winter he lived on
His track betrayed a gimp

The next fall, his rack was malformed
And he did not look fit
Winter was hard, we had few hopes
But somehow he made it

For two more winters he survived
His antlers still showed stress
But Boots each year with different does
Had passed a better test

We hadn't fed the deer for years
Wasting disease a fear
But feeder seeds that birds knocked down
Old Boots considered dear

Sometimes he stood on his hind legs
And bumped a feeder high
He often got sunflower treats
Like manna from the sky

His antlers then, before they shed
Let him do bump and run
One year a feeder knocked one off
He was left with just one

Shaped like a pronghorn's unique rack
The antler like its twin
Was thick and sturdy for its size
With substance – just like him

PASSING THE BUCK

Two shots ring out across the lake
They resonate, reverberate
Deer hunting season has begun
The rut is on, deer on the run

Old cars and trucks pull off the road
Disgorge hunters the woods enfold
They sit in tree stands for long hours
Survey below like higher powers

Blaze orange reflects from falling snow
And from white on the ground below
Deer hunter trails show their fresh tracks
In darkness, they'll follow them back

Some hunt for trophies, some for meat
Some love the woods, outdoors a treat
Others see shacks and fellowship
As most important on their trips

Tradition plays a hefty part
Each generation gets a start
We pass the hunting ethic on
To nieces, nephews, daughters, sons

Stories, hot spots, tricks of the trade
Guns and ammo, stands we have made
Blaze orange clothing, camouflage too
Doe scent, rattles, just what to do

In papers now we often see
Pictures of first hunts – kids' trophies
The biggest bucks get lots of press
Family values at their best

But hunters have another role
They help keep deer herds in control
Car accidents may be reduced
And deer-related forest abuse

We know too, that our moose decline
Where whitetail numbers do grow high
Brainworms where species overlap
Cause moose to die; deer take the rap

Reducing deer herds means that does
Should be preferred as shooting goes
So let's hand down wise use for luck
Shoot more fat does, pass on some bucks

STRANGERS IN THE NIGHT

When your home is in the North Woods
Bats may come closer than they should
They like to roost inside your house
But make more noise than the odd mouse

Most noise is quite ultrasonic
But bat presence can be chronic
They scamper as they come and go
Their hours are odd, wouldn't you know?

Little brown bats migrate each year
Arriving when warm weather's near
Some hibernate through coldest times
In fall, most leave for warmer climes

Bats mate in fall, give birth in spring
Flying pregnant is not their thing
Somehow females can store live sperm
All winter long, then come to term

Lone male bats roost somewhere outside
But female groups in houses hide
Only one pup each year is reared
But twice the bats is to be feared

Bats in your house can be okay
Until the ceiling walks away
Females come back, return to pups
Moving around when you're not up

So, as the moms and kids increased
Warm hospitality did cease
We watched the bats at three a.m.
To find the house holes used by them

We caulked all holes that we could find
Except a couple left behind
In those, one-way doors to install
So bats can exit in the fall

For that's when young are on the wing
And bats fly out but not back in
They'll have to find another house
Before they make their fall trip south

No bats were harmed in this short poem
But they are now out of our home
And when they're outside and not in
I like to think both species win

WOOD WORK

Three cords of wood had been cut down
From near Stump Lake just east of town
Though timber prices were not high
Firewood costs were through the sky

Still, propane prices were much worse
So we invested in wood first
For winter comfort down the line
In a bear climate, we'll be fine

A six-ton truck brought us some wood
Split birch and maple, looking good
The driver dumped it near our shed
Took lots of money, then he fled

Our bin was only ten by ten
We knew we'd fill it, but by when?
The pile of wood stretched far and wide
We hoped it all would fit inside

The logs were wet and heavy too
And rain had started, right on cue
Some pieces showed a lovely grain
Made more distinct by falling rain

Sapsucker holes in a few birch
But no decay; could have been worse
It still had lots of BTUs
When dry, there would be heat we'd use

Some outdoor smells clung to our clothes
From handling pieces that we chose
We picked up logs but many slipped
Our wet and cold hands lost their grips

We stacked logs up to seven feet
Completing each row was a treat
With spaces for bats, mice and bugs
A chipmunk watched the logs we lugged

And spaces in-between the chunks
Provided more than tiny bunks
The wood would dry a year or two
Thanks to the air that could blow through

It took us just about three hours
To stack three cords with senior power
We shivered under gray fall skies
But good hard work does satisfy

I'm sure a couple years from now
We'll think of what we did and how
The energy we used then will
Be paid back in low heating bills

HIGH TIMES

There is a place where birders go
That might surprise those who don't know
A spot that is not in good taste
In fact, some say it is a waste

A sewage lagoon pond may smell
But traveling birdlife know it well
And when they leave, they leave refreshed
Though their diet there may not seem best

The nutrients in sewage sludge
Grow plants birds eat – and lots of bugs
Some flies come in drawn by the smell
And some birds find the swill just swell

Upon a breezy autumn day
(Which blew some odor far away)
Cedar waxwings were catching flies
Over a pond on every try

Dozens of birds on a fence wire
Striped young and old, they did not tire
Each flew into a brisk west wind
Snapped up a fly, landed again

Repeatedly, each sallied out
The bugs they caught would fly them south
Yellow wax in bright sunshine
More fat inside them as they dined

Sandpipers – yellowlegs and least
Also came to join the feast
Adding fat for the long trips out
To South America, no doubt

Spotted sandpipers were there too
Bobbing along in shoreline goo
The bugs they caught – just like fast food
Expedient, if you're in the mood

Waterfowl of many species
Swam in water extra greasy
Mallards, gadwalls and goldeneyes
Wood ducks and teal of smaller size

Red-tailed hawks and turkey vultures
Hung around the toxic culture
Drawn by a sense of death and life
High overhead like living kites

Tree swallows, at home in the breeze
Crisscrossed the ponds with graceful ease
Catching bugs where there were plenty
One could hardly call it hunting

Ring-billed gulls buoyantly floated
Bonaparte's we also noted
So white atop the pollution
Pre-immersion absolution

I'd say high times were had by all
That aromatic day in fall
So when the birds come back next spring
We'll visit sewage ponds again

WEED WALK

One autumn day, I thought I'd go
Where pearly everlastings grow
With large-leafed asters by the road
Long-lasting blooms, flowers I know

Old bracken fern, wrinkled and brown
Enduring too, but all scrunched down
No sign of life remaining there
Foretelling winter, cold and bare

Clover heads also, shriveled, gray
Once flushed with pink a summer's day
Lupine pods twisted open, brown
Seeds flung from capsules to the ground

Thistles not colored purple now
And lacking silky thistledown
With nothing to redeem their spines
Save goldfinch nests their silk now lines

Goldenrod with pale yellow heads
Once showy and indeed widespread
So sparse now, if it's seen at all
A few plants show round insect galls

Flat yarrow and Queen Anne's lace heads
No longer white, but brown instead
Lace folded into bird's nest knobs
Like tiny scepters or hair bobs

Tall golden reed canary grass
Long pointed leaves, heads barely last
Plantain, in contrast, hugs the earth
But to long seed heads gives new birth

Some spotted knapweed still in flower
Purple, but fading by the hour
And dock of several different types
Dark brown or black stalks overripe

Such ruderal plants – weeds seen each fall
Are better than no plants at all
They thrive in places humans use
And soften barren spots abused

AUTUMN PASSAGE

The Boundary Waters in the fall
When leaves begin to turn
Is arguably the best of all
At least, that's what I've learned

The water's warm, the nights are chilled
The days are often fair
The wind can challenge, even thrill
A paddling test out there

Solo canoes are often seen
Most folks seem out to fish
So if toward solitude you lean
You may just get your wish

Small insects are not bothersome
The air is crisp and clean
Migrating birds starting to come
Viewscapes stretch like a dream

Goose calls are heard high in the sky
Birds on their southward trek
A sharp-shinned hawk flaps and glides by
She's not far off the deck

Loon families swim in threes or fours
Young ones now hunt alone
Some on mid-lake and some near shore
They'll soon leave summer's home

The loons just watch as you glide close
Less flighty than in spring
Their chicks now grown, they seem to pose
In peace that autumn brings

Mergansers in long sneaky lines
Swim hidden in shadows
Their families too, seem less to mind
When our canoes drift close

Bald eagles twitter in tree tops
Their wimpy voices raised
On flattened wings their long glides stop
With slow flaps as we gaze

The rut is on now for the moose
We hear some nighttime grunts
It's good to know they're hanging loose
Just weeks before the hunt

Chipmunks, red squirrels and gray jays too
Companions in our camp
Less there for us than for our food
Like moths drawn to a lamp

A beaver slaps its flattened tail
Across the wavy lake
Skies red, as daylight starts to fail
It seems just for our sake

After dark, waves break on the shore
We rest in cozy tents
With loon song outside, who needs more?
Our time has been well spent

MAHNOMEN

The people come from far and near
To harvest wild rice with their gear
It's not much past the break of day
As two by two they reach the bay

Each with canoe pushed from the rear
By a good punter who can steer
To places rice is ripe and thick
Go slow and steady, that's the trick

Smooth push-pole, fifteen feet in length
Cedar with light, enduring strength
One end a "duckbill" to push off
So it won't sink in, cause rice loss

The second person in the craft
Sits on the bottom, toward the aft
Facing forward; canoe a "bowl"
To fill with wild rice as they go

Two tapered sticks to flail rice heads
One pulls them over the boat bed
The other knocks rice to the floor
Each kernel stripped makes that much more

Green grain springs back with stalks upright
Intact, until kernels grow ripe
For harvest at a later date,
Or feeds wildlife, or germinates

While ricers use mahnomen beds
Fat coots find someplace else instead
It's hard to say how many leave
Each afternoon there's a reprieve

And walleyes too, may alter range
Disturbed by temporary change
But I doubt the effect is great
Few ricers remain in our state

Six hours go by, ricers ashore
Some canoes filled, some could hold more
Folks scoop up rice in feed mill sacks
Hundreds of pounds to carry back

Worth perhaps two bucks for each pound
Much more if processed, all around
Parched, threshed and winnowed for your use
Rice can get pricey, that's the truth

But boy, it sure tastes good with fish
In soup or hot dish, should you wish
And ricing gives one a big lift
Like the mahnomen, it's a gift

RAILS IN THE RICE

Autumn twilight in the rice marsh
Human harvesters nearly done
Rice flailed to be winnowed and parched
Or submerged beneath upright stalks

Rice boats have carved in grassy beds
Watery trails for swimming ducks
But some birds fly straight in instead
And swim through plant stems anywhere

A bittern flies from left to right
Slow, strong wingbeats atop the grass
In failing light before the night
Then drops and disappears from view

A great blue heron stands stock-still
Until it sees me come too close
Then it lowers body and bill
And moves slowly along the bed

A plaintive call sounds from the north
In distant wild rice on the lake
At once, squat shapes move back and forth
Close to my feet, the soras skulk

They work shoreline and the shallows
Searching for rice before they sleep
I see many of these fellows
As thick fog and darkness descend

Some rise, their bodies hovering low
Tilted stem to stern in short flight
Legs dangling, laboring as they go
They plop in water as they land

More birds fly farther out from shore
In fading light, I scarce see all
Numerous now, there must be scores
Dark shapes out in the rice marsh roost

Their numbers build up as they stage
Storing up fat for long flights south
They've been here now for several days
Cold weather will soon push them on

They migrate at night, wings not weak
To southern climes and winter range
From our Gulf shores to Caribbean
From Mexico to countries south

Though it's not spring a whinny rings
Across the marsh and in the night
Descending as it fades and brings
A farewell to the day and fall

TO THE BIG LAKE IN LATE FALL

Lake Superior on the North Shore
Autumn's bright colors are no more
The air is frigid and the wind
And people are less out than in

On ancient lava, great waves break
Chilled waters make me ponder fate
Gales of November, lives long lost
Commercial ships – goods at great cost

Ojibwe once came by canoe
At first a few, their numbers grew
They fished and hunted, planted food
Life was not easy but was good

Explorers, traders, followed them
Then settlers stayed where none had been
Commercial fishing, mining came
Invasive species, shipping lanes

Lighthouses vital to this coast
Now tourists visit them at most
Their keepers watched the waters vast
Most lights now relics of the past

Today a laker heads for port
A long and low-slung rusty sort
My dad once worked on such a boat
And left behind a log he wrote

The lonely cobbled beaches stretch
With rounded stones – a thought they fetch
Of power made manifest in time
Slow change wrought, no less sublime

Blue basalt and red rhyolite
Quartz crystals sparkle in the light
Hard agate pieces on the ground
Found after storms by some rockhounds

The big surf booms, a rhythmic bass
The small stones shift from place to place
They murmur, forming ridge and trough
The strong winds whistle on and off

White gulls still rest on wharfs and spits
They squabble, scream and sometimes fish
Their grace displayed on open wing
Can make their din more welcoming

Sea ducks have come down from the north
Old squaws and scoters, all three sorts
Harlequin ducks are far from rare
I scan the waves to see my share

Buntings, larks, longspurs have arrived
Synchronized flocks, themselves alive
Light-colored, they foretell the snow
Whirling along, soon south they'll go

Gray white-tailed deer to be pursued
Grouse hunters just part of the mood
Fisher folk between the seasons
We all brave cold for different reasons

The dark waves chase the leaden sky
They rise to greet it; who knows why
The far horizon's where they meet
A timeless play, staged at my feet

SUCKER HOLE ?

Layers of gray clouds, of darkening hue
Suggest a storm is nigh
But morning light streams strongly through
A blue hole in the sky

Around the pink horizon's rim
Some light supports the dark
The subdued hope barely creeps in
It fails to make its mark

Now through the hole in falling beams
Light touches Mother Earth
Like waterfalls in endless streams
Continuous rebirth

We place some hope in sucker holes
Such fleeting spots of blue
They all too often fail to grow
Just when we want them to

But when blue skies push back the clouds
We are cheered by the sun
A bit more light, a bit less doubt
We are no longer glum

Light beams aren't something we can climb
We earthlings can't ascend
So that which brings us brighter times
Must from on high descend

A PERFECT STONE

I walk the cobbled beach alone
As I look for a perfect stone
The beach washed by waves from the lake
She'll never miss what I might take

Three terraces along the shore
Formed when the waves were less or more
I walk the lowest one not wet
Others may not have searched it yet

I don't know much geology
But I can tell what pleases me:
Basalt made smooth by water wear
Stones of odd color, here and there

Or heavy granite paperweights
A worry stone to ponder fate
Rhyolite, pink as baby's butt
Quartz glistening in a vein uncut

A banded agate in rock chink
Thompsonite with green and pink
Stones purple, or brown, speckled white
And two-toned rocks – part dark, part light

But all stones harbor some "defects"
Cracks, gas pock marks – they're not perfect
Or could it be that, as some say
Each is a gem in its own way?

"Perfect" is only in the mind
Whether for stones or humankind
Folks in our lives, stones on the beach
Let's value those within our reach

AUTUMN WAVES

Great waves on Lake Superior's shore
No land behind them as they come
Perpetual – each one breeds still more
From depths unlikely to be plumbed

Rising near lichen-spotted rock
They turn from black to jaded green
Tremendous power held half-cocked
As light behind their power's seen

Some spend themselves on stone not soft
Crags that rise steep near lava worn
And send white spray to hang aloft
Each droplet from wave newly born

The cold north wind, on this fall day
Fair chills all creatures to the bone
But carvings from time's endless waves
Give some water a placid home

Crevasses, pits and fissured stone
Hold water and gold leaves of fall
Aspen or willow – grouped, alone
Wait wet or dry for winter's call

And there a lengthy lava ridge
Provides a sloping shoreward side
To make a spillway at its edge
So liquid in thin fans can glide

Spruce, fir and cedar, dwarfed and thin
Find spots to pierce the lava bench
Red berries hang on naked limbs
Sphagnum and grasses join the dance

A laker under heavy skies
Heads for this water-troubled shore
So distant is it to my eyes
I see its outline, nothing more

Tomorrow's snow is in the air
As autumn draws now to a close
Things that endure in life are rare
In time, even the rocks erode

CHANGE YOU CAN BELIEVE IN

I saw a brick-red buck today
Knee deep in lime-green ferns
The autumn is upon us, yet
His coat has not yet turned

Deer winter coats are much more drab
Hair warmer, thicker, gray
More suited to harsh winter life
With shorter, darker days

The brown coats of the snowshoe hare
Are changing to pure white
In autumn, there are some of both
On the hares that you sight

And in the fall, a predator
Prepares for the season
Short-tailed weasel fur turns white too
Camouflage, a reason

Now, hair and feathers that are white
Lack pigment grains within
So hold more insulating air
Cold stays out and heat in

Ruffed grouse and hares change their shoe size
They grow "combs" and foot hair
For better walking on deep snow
No sinking feelings there

Some mammals add more body fat
Raise metabolic rates
If they can maintain body heat
No need to hibernate

Some decrease body temps so far
Tissues may nearly freeze
If outside temperatures get low
They wake or they decease

In autumn, bears gorge, put on fat
To use up when they den
Their body temps remain quite high
Though they don't eat again

Nor do they drink or urinate
Or produce toxic waste
While in the den, they can be roused
And they lose lots of weight

Cholesterol, twice what it was
Bears don't lose muscle mass
Show diabetes or bone loss
Though exercise they lack

Our flying squirrels like to huddle
In small groups and warm nests
Red squirrels horde food and stay wakeful
Fur thickened for cold tests

Chipmunks store seeds in their larders
To cut down on cold sleep
For when they waken from torpor
There's something there to eat

Gray jays store food for winter use
They gorge on autumn days
Saliva from large glands is used
To protect pellets made

Chickadees get fat when it's light
Lose it shivering in bursts
They lower body temps at night
As weather does its worst

They pick out spots for overnight
Small ones, protection's lent
They roost alone, but may be cramped
Come morning, tails are bent

Siskins, redpolls and goldfinches
Grow more autumn feathers
Twice the number as in summer
To fluff in colder weather

Frogs and insects change things too
As small ice crystals form
But only in-between their cells
Cell tissues kept from harm

Most frogs use glucose in their cells
Insects use glycerol
Antifreeze lowers freezing points
And it's changed in the fall!

Fish use a different antifreeze
With proteins in their cells
And seek warmer water below
When lakes turn over well

It's clear that autumn can bring change
If you don't migrate south
Like plants, animals must adapt
Through change inside and out

So next time foliage colors up,
Light fades and cold appears
Recall that all life has to change
To live year-round up here

TREE THOUGHTS

The bracken fern, long rusty brown
Red sumac now joins in
Aspen and birch, yellow and gold
The woods begin to thin

Changed maples too, stand here and there
Some scarlet against green
Beneath the gray and gloomy clouds
They demand to be seen

Bright painted leaves float gently down
Caught by a wayward breeze
They start a carpet on the ground
A loose but pleasant weave

Balsams, unchanged for what's ahead
Stand tall amidst the pines
Lichen-encrusted, brittle things
Most linger past their prime

Downed birch, aspen and balsam trees
Litter the forest floor
Riddled by insects and disease
Most rotten to the core

As I chop wood for next year's warmth
My thoughts are much on trees
Like other things in life, I guess
They bother and they please

AUTUMNAL VIEWS

It strikes me that sometimes in fall
When some leaves have turned, but not all
Nature is mostly green and gold
Like Green Bay Packers in the cold

Maroon and gold can be seen too
Though not as often, it is true
So Minnesota has its day
But in a more collegiate way

Purple with white is hard to find
Our Vikings do not come to mind
It's just as well in recent years
When watching them is fraught with fears

Some Bronco orange and Redskin red
Are now found here up north instead
And Cleveland's brown as seen in oaks
Is less familiar to most folks

But nature's colors are to share
Not to divide by what we wear
Often, our human divisions
Strongly color our decisions

HONK IF YOU LOVE AUTUMN

Black clots in gray autumnal skies
Resolving now in my mind's eye
Large waterfowl in lines and vees
Approaching slowly, at their ease

Increasing numbers come in view
At closer range, still in dark hue
The far horizon offers more
Not just a few, but by the score

Their numbers exceed local flocks
They're here on a refueling stop
Refuge and potholes all about
Protect them as they travel south

Sunflowers and corn stand in the fields
Some waste escapes the farmers' yields
Migrant geese on their feeding flights
Have left safe havens of last night

Wild geese aren't rare here in the north
You see and hear their back and forth
It makes you wonder where they've been
When they will go and come again

Geese boldly connect north and south
Through sky-high flights and word of mouth
And let us know fall's in full swing
When they move southward on the wing

THREE SWANS

Three tundra swans just passed me by
White bodies glistening in dawn light
Long necks stretched southward in the sky
In graceful migratory flight

In the far north, in North Dakota
Skim ice is forming everywhere
More swans massed in Minnesota
On Mississippi waters there

A few are feeding – tipping up
White bottoms stuck up in cold air
Young birds and old together sup
On water plants, their submerged fare

Down from the arctic heath they've come
From nesting grounds on raised sedge hills
Some are taken by hunters' guns
But swans no longer should be killed

The old birds know the way back east
They key on valleys, rivers, lakes
As they move on to Chesapeake
With few refueling stops to make

For those that reach the salty brine
A seaside life will be in store
As they rest up for breeding time
And the long flight up north once more

FREAK OUT OR SNEAK OUT ?

A chuckle near the trail ahead
In the tall grass, a feathered head
A ruffed grouse exiting the woods
Displaying caution, as one should

As the path moved – or was it bird?
(The pace so slow it was absurd)
Two other heads appeared behind
In single file – heads of one kind

Nearby in red pine near to us
A red squirrel tried, but couldn't fuss
He jerked his tail and twitched around
But he did not utter a sound

He had a pine cone in his teeth
(You shouldn't chatter while you eat)
His rage was muted with no scolds
But his demeanor no less bold

We turned again to our slow birds
As a few sounds from them we heard
Now there were eight, all single file
Four on each side of path's wide aisle

Some glacial progress, but one change
Each wildly ran across the lane
But slowed down on the other side
Torsos, not heads, the grass could hide

Time crossing trail? Thirty minutes
More, if you count grass-time in it
If time flies when you're having fun
The grouse were having close to none

Meanwhile, our squirrel had found his voice
His pine cone stashed, that was his choice
He scolded us without pine cone
We still were in his "it's my zone"

And as we moved slowly away
Eight grouse flushed noisily that day
The sound of wing whirs filled the air
But we were glad they had been there

OCTOBER KAYAKING

After a month of wind and rain
Comes a calm windfall of a day
At the tag end of a cold fall
A clear morning past resisting

Spider webs inside the kayaks
Pollen and bird droppings outside
Rain has raised lake water levels
The kayaks slide smoothly in

It is late in the afternoon
Despite the absence of a breeze
We feel the chill in the shade
The water is cold to the touch

In the low light against the sun
We see two loons in silhouette
Still calling on our small lake
Not yet grouped up on big water

People aren't ready for winter
Docks are still down and lawn chairs out
Voices carry across the water
Summer people are still up north

Shoreline cedars hold their skirts high
Above the placid water's surface
Like a big city chorus line
From a kayaker's perspective

My paddle disturbs a turtle
Floating just beneath the surface
Surprised, it splashes as it dives
Thumping the paddle as it goes

As we approach the small island
The two loons appear at the point
They give tremolo calls and dive
Disturbed by our distant approach

We slow to a glide, they surface
Then call again and dive twice more
Suddenly they are behind us
And their calls now seem like laughter

As we ease into the still pond
A beaver slaps its tail and dives
Disturbing the air and water
Causing us to stop in mid-stroke

So easily in the high water
The kayaks slide out on the dock
We hope for another outing
But in October who can say?

SMOKY GOLD

It is the time of smoky gold
Before the weather grows too cold
The swamps and bogs now look their best
Indians recall an ancient test:

Chickadee, lest he come to harm
Asked Larch for branches to keep warm
But this proud tree with shape so fine
Said, "You can't have them; they are mine"

Great Spirit saw and told the tree
"Now you must die with your fine leaves"
Chickadee said, "Please let him live"
"Okay, but his leaves he must give"

These "evergreens" that drop their leaves
Live farther north than other trees
They don't do well in others' shade
But in poor soils they have it made

In wintertime, less water there
With frozen ground and bone-dry air
Without leaves, tamaracks retain
Their moisture with less loss, no gain

Smoky gold color says it all
For prior to the end of fall
Gold needles drop from every branch
Undressing trees for winter's dance

IN-BETWEEN TIME

How tan and gray the landscape seems
We drive through it as in a dream
The crops are in, stubble remains
All that is left of summer's gain

The prairie dry, the birds are gone
Farmsteads and fallow fields forlorn
No people there, where do they go?
Are they now south, do they lie low?

Tree branches black, skeletons bare
Punctuate skylines here and there
Brooding clouds pout, swollen and low
Warning the land it's soon to snow

In this bland time of in-between
I guess I miss both white and green
But there is value in the pause
Between what's coming and what was

WITHOUT
SPECIAL
SEASONING

THE MILKY WAY

Our galaxy the Milky Way
Is a big disc from far away
A spiral like a ninja star
Four major arms spreading out far

Two hundred billion stars or more
I wonder who is keeping score
But break it down I guess we must
There's also gas, black holes and dust

It gives me pause each time I say
It's thirteen billion years in age
Some stars old as the universe
Our galaxy among the first

And it's twelve thousand light-years thick
You count the gas too, that's the trick
One hundred thousand light-years long
My grasp of that is not too strong

But if it helps, a light-year is
Six trillion miles, come hit or miss
I still can't fathom what that means
I'm not as bright as those light beams

And ninety-three million miles from earth
Our sun revolves, for what it's worth
Around the central Milky Way
And drags us with it night and day

The Milky Way gives out dim light
It's hard to see from town at night
But it's there year round, right or wrong
The sky split in hemispheres long

Greek myth has it the Milky Way
Is Hera's milk spilled as she lay
Suckling Hercules in the sky
We probably need not ask why

Some people think it is the path
For the deads' souls – the aftermath
So souls don't really have to roam
Far from the earth on their way home

To others it's a river wide
To hunt along, perhaps to ride
For gods and goddesses and men
As they enjoy good life again

But what I see when I look up
Is a sweet stream from brimming cup
Of starlight in the Milky Way
To drink in after a long day

OVER THE MOON

A cool night-light in endless sky
Reflecting sunlight to our eyes
So bright it can dim distant stars
Whose true lights burn, though from afar

Moonshine bounces from our moon's face
To earth's surface and human race
And "earthshine" sometimes lights the moon
They both dance to the sun's bright tune

Four and one-half billion years old
The size of Africa, we're told
As large as the Pacific's Basin
Our deepest ocean – that's amazin'!

The moon sprung forth from a collision
Earth struck by meteor, that's the vision
And now the moon orbits the earth
Attracted to what gave it birth

Our natural satellite so fine
Keeps full and new and quarter time
In twenty-nine days it revolves
Around the earth, phases resolved

Daily time Luna tells is true
Just watch her phases for your cue
Each rises, sets in time and place
Established as the earth rotates

And tidal time, both high and low
Proof that the moon attracts us so
About twelve hours between each high
As near and far our oceans rise

As earth rotates its oceans bulge
Gravity sucks, I can divulge
The earth farthest from the moon's force
Is pulled less; oceans too, of course

Sun and moon aligned give reason
"Spring" tides are not just at one season
Their water rises strong and high
And in-between come weak "neap" tides

We always see the moon's near side
It stays turned toward us as we ride
A moon-day long as an earth-month
Revolve and rotate all at once

The moon's far side – not always dark
Although both sides define what's stark
But at new moon when we've no light
The far side of the moon is bright

Light-colored highlands and dark "seas"
Craters from impacts of debris
Give us some features to abstract
Into good stories or a map

Some people see two eyes, a smile
"The man in the moon" for a while
Or there's a hare or toad sometimes
Others make up some nursery rhymes

At full moon, two kids on a climb
Young Jack and Jill are side by side
They hold a pail there in-between
To fetch water from lunar seas

By third quarter, Jack's fallen down
At waning crescent, Jill is gone
They don't succeed, but they will mend
And next month they can try again

The moon's orbit – not quite the same
As the earth's own ecliptic plane
Where they intersect is a node
Eclipses occur – different modes

Our moon is high in winter months
Because earth tips away from sun
In summertime, Luna hangs low
Then earth points toward the sun, you know

And the moon can seem to change when
Its orbit brings it close to men
Or next to objects here on earth
It appears larger in its girth

If you want to see its real size
Bend down and with inverted eyes
Look at our Luna upside down
Mooning the moon – it helps somehow

What the moon brings to life on earth
From migration to spawn and birth
To honeymooners, lunatics
We also should add to the mix

And if the moon needs further voice
The common loon would be my choice
Crazy, unique and undefiled
The song of one alone and wild

NORTHERN LIGHTS

Like Christo's curtains in the sky
Out-of-place candy for the eye
Moving, dancing colors that float
Aristotle saw jumping goats

Valkyries in long painted gowns
Bring home dead warriors they have found
Goddesses drag their colored trains
And men home to Odin again

Ancestors happy way up there
Celebrate, play in the cold air
Shamans who visit in trances know
That is where the dead souls go

Some say the light from summer sun
Issues from glaciers in dark months
Or that the holes in mountainsides
Release steam from bright fire inside

Inuit, Saami, other folks
Know it is not wise to provoke
The Lights or you may turn to stone
Best not to go out all alone

And some say that Lights come when called
To bring good luck to one and all
Others throw rocks to split in two
What brings bad weather down on you

As wondrous as all of that sounds
It cannot top what science has found
For it all starts out on our sun
As spots and flares form one by one

The flares so high they dwarf the earth
Helium burning, giving birth
To solar wind that blows our way
Charged plasma gas both night and day

But earth has a magnetosphere
That keeps us from some things we fear
Force fields from our magnetic poles
Miles beyond earth in space, we're told

Most plasma is deflected by
But some leaks in to please the eye
It speeds up, strikes gas in our air
Nitrogen, oxygen up there

And these charged gases then yield light
Greens, reds and blues – it's quite a sight
Charged atoms that circle the poles
Arranging, changing, like lost souls

The Lights themselves can stop our power
Induce magnetic fields for hours
Brain cancer another result
Heart healing is brought to a halt

I guess we're lucky Northern Lights
Are circumpolar, hard to sight
Sent from long cycles of the sun
And miles above 'most everyone

But though I've seen some green lights here
I long for curtains, colors; fear
That until I go farther north
Such magic sights will not come forth

Maybe some fall, winter or spring
I'll do some midnight wandering
Amid the polar bears and snow
In search of nature's high light show

CLOUDS *

Yes, "Rows and floes of angel hair
And ice-cream castles in the air"
I've looked at clouds in that way too
But here's another point of view

Clouds are nothing, if they're not change
They grow, disperse and rearrange
They're high and low and in-between
And ten groups of them may be seen

1. CUMULUS

Like cotton candy in the sky
One by one these puffy clouds rise
From moisture in warm air near earth
On blue-sky morns they're given birth

You see them on fair-weather days
Low in the sky, not far away
They may build up into tall towers
Or drift gently along for hours

Their bases are quite well defined
To the same altitude they climb
They sometimes bring us a brief rain
More if they swell before midday

2. CUMULONIMBUS

The "King of Clouds" builds up so high
Through trophosphere this cloud can rise
Updrafts and downdrafts deep within
Thunder and lightning – thrilling twins

A storm cloud in the strictest sense
With hail and snow and rain most dense
Ice crystals high in anvil crown
Which spreads out far, attracts a crowd

Lightning bolts flash – mostly within
Some go to earth, some back again
And lightning jumps from cloud to cloud
Or to the outside air around

3. STRATUS

Like a gray blanket overhead
With little rain or snow in stead
A stratus cloud can stay for days
In stable air it blocks sun rays

Our lowest cloud, close to the ground
It tends to bring some people down
The only cloud we can walk through
It comes as mist and as fog too

In low spots that can grow cold fast
Then warm as nightly cooling's past
O'er water warm in air that's cold
"Sea smoke" is seen where cool air flows

4. STRATOCUMULUS

With air inversions, cumulus clouds
Cannot rise far, thus start to crowd
Stratus clouds rumpled by the wind
Are unstable; thermals begin

In these and several other ways
Such clouds can form both white and gray
They may pick up heat from the ground
Expand and float up all around

They don't hold lots of rain or snow
Take more shapes than most clouds so low
Some look like castles in the air
The Greeks dreamed of fine cities there

5. ALTOCUMULUS

Up high, above the thermal zone
Altocumulus makes its home
Comprised of cloudlets in the air
Whether in patches or in layers

Cloudlets equal in shape and size
They look best near sunset and -rise
Spaced out in patches, rolls or balls
They rarely cause much rain to fall

These clouds are found about mid-height
The cloudlets are both gray and white
Unlike such forms that are up high
These clouds are larger, not of ice

6. ALTOSTRATUS

These higher clouds are thick or thin
Moisture or not for us within
They can be dark or a blue-white
Sun and moon may shine through them bright

Altostratus are like gray shrouds
Much like the lower stratus clouds
They are called boring clouds by some
Corona discs show obscured sun

When it is time for dawn or dusk
The sun shines under this stratus
If red at dusk, coming skies clear
If red at dawn, more clouds to fear

Since weather arrives from the west
No clouds are there to block sunset
At dawn, red skies mean all clear east
But in the west fair skies will cease

7. NIMBOSTRATUS

A thick gray blanket low to high
This cloud will spread out far and wide
A cloud so dense it blocks the sun
It holds moisture for everyone

Nimbus – the Latin word for rain
But not a cloudburst – it's sustained
It rains or snows for hours or days
And doesn't want to go away

Rain obscures and hides what's in it
It's hard to find a lower limit
Snow or ice storms can blur it too
This stratus gives us all its due

8. CIRRUS

In high white patches, streaks or bands
They don't hold rain, they just look grand
So high they're made of falling ice
Which doesn't reach earth, and that's nice

You can find "mare's-tails", "angel hair"
Or silk threads spun into the air
They are detached, take up some room
Form halos around sun or moon

They're moved by high winds that are strong
And don't remain in one place long
But since they are so far away
They look to us as if they stay

When these clouds thicken and spread out
There's rising warmer air about
Low pressure cells are moving in
The rain comes soon – it's depressing

But at the end of moister air
The sky is cleaner everywhere
Come colder air and winds of storms
Cumulonimbus towers form

9. CIRROCUMULUS

These high clouds appear as fine grains
In patches that do not show shade
"Mackerel sky" is another name
Altocum' not the same

Though mackerel sky is cloudlets too
They're smaller grained than altocum'
The ripples of a mackerel sky
With mare's-tails mean a storm is nigh

The mare's-tails tell us winds are strong
Depression and rain before long
With cirrocum' clouds in the sky
There is much moisture carried high

But mackerel sky may soon dissolve
Or turn to cirrostratus fog
Or hang out there with other types
Of cirrus clouds up at that height

10. CIRROSTRATUS

High milky veils, crystals of ice
So subtle that we must look twice
Though they can cover lots of sky
They're most known for effects we spy

Colored halos 'round moon or sun
"Sundogs" come in pairs, not just one
Effects of crystals in the clouds
And how they fall, bend light around

Crystalline "grins" high in the air
"Cloud smiles" are rainbows way up there
(Most true rainbows are formed low down
From liquid water near the ground)

Reflections from ice crystal faces
Cause "sun pillars" in two places
Broad bright lines above or below
A partial frame when sun is low

Well, Joni Mitchell's "both sides" song
Does make me want to sing along
But though illusions can be nice
I like my clouds with rain and ice

* With thanks to: G. Preter-Pinney, *The Cloudspotter's Guide*, Perigree Books, New York, 2006; J.A. Day, *The Book of Clouds*, Sterling Publishing Co., Inc., New York, 2006; and Joni Mitchell, *Both Sides Now*, 1968.

STONE STORIES *

When you're canoeing northern lakes
Or paddling cold clear streams
You're sometimes dwarfed by high rock walls
Straight up – most do not lean

If you look closely as you glide
You may see spots of red
They could be lichen on the rock
Or pictographs instead

The ochre used for this fine art
Is powdered hematite
With fish-oil base or egg, they say
To make the paint stick tight

In fact, it binds right to the rock
Endures for centuries
Without peeling or flaking off
Though vandalized with ease

Anishinabe ancestors
More recent peoples too
Painted the rock several feet up
While standing in canoes

They did it to create, some say
Or record derring-do
Or talk to other passersby
On snowshoes, in canoes

166

Perhaps some shamans painted rocks
To reach the spirit world
Called out the game for men to hunt
Fishes from where they lurked

Thunderbirds that they painted there
Reside up in the sky
The Panther, a great water god
Could drown you if he tried

Some little men who steal your fish
And hide out in rock cracks
Canoes bound for the spirit world
Moose with gigantic racks

There are dozens of these art groups
Painted near watery routes
In Canada and the U.S.
Worth exclaiming about

I've been to many in my life
But one group's in my mind
The pictographs at Hegman Lake
Among the best you'll find

They tell a story, if you'll hear
About a people's way
With earth and sky and wildlife too
And here is what they say

Orion, the Wintermaker
Great Panther and the Moose
Ojibwe constellations bold
Are painted in this group

The Moose is also our Great Square
In fall and wintertime
It shines on hunters in their camps
As on big game they dine

Orion ascends the winter sky
Foretells the winter hunts
The natives once made hunting camps
For six long winter months

But when the Great Panther is seen
In March, near spring solstice
He brings with him the springtime floods
A sign people can trust

Then the Anishinabe knew
By starwork on the stone
That they must move from winter camps
Lest ice access be gone

High time for people to move out
To summer camps elsewhere
To sugarbush and fish and fowl
Then rice and berries there

Though Fisher is not at this site
(Our Big Dipper writ large)
The legends say he freed the birds
From prison in the stars

In spring he's seen upon on his back
Around the North Star's light
As if he's falling from the sky
And Fisher's stars are bright

Did the people see his long fall
Down from the sky at night
And dream of birds soon coming north
In spring migration flight?

What other tales are to be told
As more rock art we sift?
I'll bet they fit the painters' world
Their lifestyles and their myths

* With thanks to R. Morton and C.
Gawboy, *Talking Rocks*, Pfeifer-
Hamilton, Duluth, MN 2000.

BIG

The aspen leaves rustle today
All are alike in golden hue
Each stand, like Dolly, cloned they say
One organism, if it's true

In a two-hundred-acre grove
There's fifty thousand parts to view
Someone counted so that we'd know
And I don't question that it's true

Which makes me think of larger beings
You can't count God or dinosaurs
One lacks carbon and can't be seen
The other's extinct, is no more

How about giant sequoia trees?
Massive plants out on the west coast
Hard to believe they came from seeds
But I don't think they weigh the most

Blue whales can weigh seventy tons
African elephants, some six
But neither is now number one
Though both are high up on the list

Australians say Great Barrier Reef
Counts as the largest living being
And planet Earth some do believe
From space one Gaia do we see

Perhaps we should go underground
To find the largest living thing
Fungal mycelia webbed around
Like some giant tangled piece of string

Two thousand acres in the dark
Hidden under Oregon earth
Not needing light to make its mark
It sporulates to give new birth

Fungi help turn rocks into soil
Recolonize earth's toxic sites
Some taste good and some disease foil
And as was said, all without light

Fungi help other things to grow
And did so on earth early on
Insects might be the last to go
But it's fungi I'd bet upon

Still, whales and aspens get my vote
To us, they're well known and immense
But all evolved life is of note
And caring for it just makes sense

GLOBAL CLIMATE CHANGE

Everyone listen, far and near!
All of us that have ears to hear!
Pay attention! I truly fear
That global climate change is here

Summers are warmer than before
The rain is harder and much more
Storms more severe – they're keeping score
Droughts longer, hear the wildfires roar!

Winters may be forever changed
Some warmer to the point of strange
With snow and rain that's rearranged
Organisms can't all change range

And glaciers melting south and north
Sea levels rising, floods of sorts
Pack ice now drifts out far from ports
Arctic explorers, trips abort

How did these changes come about?
A winter jet stream won't go south
And ocean currents took new routes
Evaporation changed storms' clouts

Greenhouse gases now on the rise
Through forest clearing, fires of size
Methane from livestock on the side
Choices we make far less than wise

Also because of CO_2
Produced by industry and you
And me, of course; not just a few
Who want more stuff in their purview

Cycles of sea ice are now marred
So we can all drive bigger cars
Polar bears drown, swimming afar
They can't catch seals from where they are

Yellowstone grizzlies may be next
Their foods uncertain, at the best
Can whitebark pine trees stand the test
High country warming with the rest?

Our moose can't take the warmth they find
Mild winters put them in a bind
Warm summers stress what young we find
Diseases increase – of all kinds

Gray jays that store their winter food
Find that it spoils before it's used
For other species and their broods
Food timing and amounts not good

As with persistent pesticides
Global impacts we can't abide
Big business, others may deride
Our role we can no longer hide

Let's burn less carbon! Start today!
Make your life greener day by day
Old habits must become passé
The human race needs a new way!

PIECE-KEEPING

A wise man said, "Don't throw away
Pieces of what you'll need some day"
And so it is with nature's world
Whose parts mankind is prone to hurl

Away, not knowing what is lost
Or concerned about what it costs
To others who are not yet born
Of us, or nature – diverse forms

So it is good to set aside
Some places that man, in his pride
And lack of knowledge cannot touch
Or if he does, it's not so much

Then Nature's nature still remains
To compare with what we have changed
To study and to understand
And serve the future needs of man

But more than that, it's only right
If we are stewards in God's sight
To use well what we are given
Not be only by dollars driven

Parks and preserves that we protect
Help us to see how parts connect
Insects, plants, frogs, birds and mammals
Other forms by man untrammeled

In our state, we have SNAs *
Nature's museums, in many ways
Over a hundred now statewide
Such areas we can view with pride

They save gene pools for future use
Protect rare species from abuse
Give us more time to understand
And educate the child called man

These islands in a human sea
Teach us what processes we need
To keep our impacts within bounds
In other places, all around

Most sites do not have hiking trails
Or other signs of man's travail
But you can gently visit them
To understand what might have been

* Scientific Natural Areas

BEWITCHED

I saw a bright orange witch's hat
Atop a young spruce tree
Some prankster no doubt placed it there
For all the world to see

What if it were a magic hat
That in the dead of night
Transformed the tree into a witch –
Now that would be a sight!

She would have no need for a broom
She straddles her own wood
In flight she'd stick to it like sap
Fly through the air, she could

My wood witch would be a good witch
One who knows right from wrong
I know she'd protect old-growth stands
So that she'd live so long

Selective cuts and some burns too
Would be high on her list
Preserving wildlife, scenic views
Some things we all would miss

She'd manage whitetails and ruffed grouse
And aspen – worthy too
Protect the rare and threatened forms
Balanced with other use

Clearcut some forest in small blocks
Diversify landscapes
By age and species, space and time
She'd manage, but not rape

She'd know just how to balance out
Consumption with wise use
Keep man and nature harmonized
Without waste or abuse

But, save the land-use guidance of
A magic forest witch
We're all left trying to agree
And therein lies the hitch!

OF BEARS AND MEN

I saw a black bear running hard
To cross an open space
Four legs extended, front and back
A graceful bounding race

He looked both ways when legs were spread
As he crossed the four lanes
Alert to cars on either side
He played a careful game

Three hefty bears ambled along
As we sat on our bikes
They gave us pause as they walked by
Though not an awful fright

Two cubs sent up our old white pine
By Mom as danger neared
It could have been a boar, or folks
They knew enough to fear

A swimming bear seen from canoe
Another magic sight
In Boundary Waters clear and cold
In daytime or moonlight

And bears that try to steal your food
As you camp out somewhere
You take precautions as need be
If you are man or bear

On horseback I've seen grizzly bears
Alaskan browns on foot
Tracks deep and wide, scats steaming fresh
Of seeds, berries and roots

White polar bears call from afar
Across the vast pack ice
I've not seen them except in zoos
Some wild ones would be nice

I know someone who studies them
Out on the Beaufort Sea
If all of us last five more years
They'll get a look at me

Why people want to touch wild bears
Or feed them from their hands
Or why we teach both disrespect
I fail to understand

As we give them our human names
Dream that they're just big pets
And try to make them part of us
I think we fail a test

Both bears and folks should keep some fear
Of what might do them harm
And we should value what is wild
Not treat it like a farm

I know a bear means more to me
If it's not tame and fat
And it's not an authentic bear
Without wild habitat

The ancients said wild ones appear
To humans who deserve
To see wild spirits in their world
A thought we should preserve

THE COLORS PURPLE

The color purple says "I rule"
With flowing robes and funny hats
It's worn by kings and churchmen who
Value power, control and all that

Or does purple our age define?
Women sport it when they are old
White-haired folks in it, past their prime
Attract attention, looking bold

Now, Mother Nature puts in time
And surely rules more than we cede
Her moods of four can be sublime
Does purple go with *autumn* leaves?

She wears fall asters, many kinds
A change from white and yellow blooms
More regal shades than one can find
A subtle beauty gone too soon

The fireweed found on disturbed spots
Covers her nakedness with grace
Striking magenta-blooming stalks
A modest covering in good taste

Small prairie clover flowers bloom low
As color climbs each tiny head
Replacing green buds row by row
Creating purple crowns instead

And thistles flower as autumn comes
Not yet the seeds that finches seek
Sharp thorns guard purple in late sun
As insects seek an autumn treat

Woodbine leaves twine their way around
A maroon garland through the green
You find them creeping near the ground
High in the trees and in-between

Sumac bushes with purplish leaves
Bear their purple fruit in clusters
More winter food for birds and beasts
Long after flowers lose their luster

The browns and purples in the trees
Accentuate fall's golds and reds
Ferns, forbs, and grasses predict freeze
Green darkened by cold air, it's said

Fringed gentians, coneflowers, bellflowers too
Show royal colors in the fall
Joe-Pye weed's purples, bee balm's hue
Brighten landscapes and show their all

Yet *spring's* the time the iris blooms
Geraniums, bluebells flower too
Moccasins color Nature's room
And violets add a pleasing hue

Summer is regal, if one looks
At clovers, coneflowers, blazing stars
Fleabane and vetch and four o'clocks
Ripe, darkened berries, near and far

Lupine there in purple patches
Lingers on stalks as flowering heads
Soon to turn to hardened caches
Of seeds that sow the ground instead

(And if you're wondering, *winter's* when
The purple of the season's in
Our lips, noses, and fingers cold
As snow, and ice, and white grow old)

Purple – our sign to celebrate
Accomplishment, end of the dance –
Marks graduation, gives things weight
It goes with pomp and circumstance

Perhaps with Nature, it's the same
She gives us purple with a grin
To show her pride and joy, this dame
Whatever season she is in

The poet said purple is a test
(The hue in nature a surprise)
A gift from God that like the rest
We joyfully should recognize

A WHITE PINE

An old white pine grows near our house
It is about eight feet around
Stout upper branches barren now
The top – eighty feet from the ground

It grew strong on that rocky site
When loggers once came to this place
Too small – diameter and height
Safe, unlike others of its race

The ravens now use balding crown
To sometimes sit and watch the day
Perhaps they too must get unwound
Before they rise and flap away

Nuthatches of red or white breast
Cling to the bark and sometimes feed
As they work down but seldom rest
A different drummer theirs to heed

Flying squirrels launch graceful downward glides
To sunflower feeders in the dark
From the pine's branches and its sides
We seldom see their nighttime arcs

Blue and gray jays hide their caches
Of seeds and suet everywhere
Chickadees too, have their stashes
In holes and crevices up there

We've seen bear cubs, danger perceived
Sent up the trunk at their mom's call
Safe out of reach when they are treed
On rough pine bark, two black fur balls

The best thing: a few times a year
In every season on nice days
The red squirrels bring a special cheer
In chases that seem largely play

Two squirrels will use the massive tree
As a broad sticky spiral path
To chase each other in a spree
Around the trunk in fun or wrath

One pursues other, then they swap
As both squirrels circle 'round the tree
For several minutes. Then they stop
Each spread out where other can't see

But one will inch around too soon
See the other, renew the chase
Then they will switch who is pursued
Continue their corkscrewing race

This pattern has gone on for years
Beyond sex, lives or just defense –
I wish the old white pine had ears
And lips to tell us what is meant

But it's enough the pine is there
And to us, entertainment brings
To others, pantry, shelter, chair
A stately, ancient living thing

A POWER LINE

A power line runs through our woods
Right angles to the road
The right-of-way on either side
Protects the current load

Terrain uneven – filled with rocks
With troughs and cresting hills
When walking, one must watch one's feet
Beware of scrapes and spills

Beneath the line in summertime
Blueberries in the sun
Ripen on bushes everywhere
Nobody eats just one

Some winters in the open space
The snow is not as deep
As in the woods on either side
Where the sun's rays don't reach

And when the snowpack does allow
An open trail there lies
It's great to snowshoe and to view
Whatever fills your eyes

The deer, like us, use travel lanes
You see their tracks year-round
And in the fall the hunters come
Good views both up and down

You sometimes see there other sign
Grouse, fox and fisher tracks
They cross or travel the fine line
On the way there and back

Merlins, broadwings and other birds
Use perches near the space
Between the woods where they build nests
And hunt or court their mates

On many clear and starry nights
The line provides a view
One hard to come by in thick woods
The owls hunt mice there too

A power line is many things
When stretched across the land
And it can bring diversity
To nature and to man

BIRDING

I enjoy watching birds, it's true
If you try, I bet you will too
You need not watch them all the time
And usually, they do not mind

Some people watch birds in their yards
That really doesn't seem too hard
Some look for birds 'most everywhere
And search for something new or rare

Binoculars and spotting scopes
Are bought by some in the fond hope
That they will have a better look
(And birders buy at least one book)

Some play bird songs so they'll attract
Birds close enough to photograph
Some use bird servers or hot lines
To lead them to rare birds to find

And yes, some folks like to keep lists
Of birds they've seen or heard or "pished"
(To Pish: make noise, to which birds come,
Often a squeak from human tongue)

Anyhow, bird lists are diverse
For counties, states, from bed and worse
Lists by the country, each foray
Each year, each month, or all your days

But you can just watch birds year-round
On almost any plot of ground
See when they come in fall or spring
And what summer and winter bring

When do the hummingbirds come back?
And crows and phoebes, or the lack
Are ospreys here when lake ice heaves?
Do warblers come before spring leaves?

Then share what you now know with friends
It's like the weather, it depends
But you'll learn more and take more walks
And have more interesting talks

Your world will widen as you learn
Think like a bird as you discern
What might impact what you observe
A forest lost, a song unheard

How a marsh drained, a parking lot
Change bird landscapes, likely as not
And how bad storms kill traveling birds
Windmills and lights too, take my word

Bird-watching can help us to see
And take responsibility
To make each other understand
How to live lightly on the land

THE BUILDER

He cut the trees from his own land
All quaking aspen, straight and tall
Barked and milled them with his hands
His only tool, an old chainsaw

He stacked the logs to age a bit
So he'd not have to use them green
Then with his helpmate hoisted them
To build the cabin he'd forseen

Just a small structure in the woods
With power, but no plumbing yet
The outhouse was a work of art
With window, varnished bench, carpet

He rigged a catchment system too
For showers and drinking water
A good wood stove to cook his food
I don't know just where he got her

A proper workshop for his tools
A shelter for tractor and truck
A woodshed for his source of fuel
Popple and birch, limbed, chopped and bucked

He built a fireplace from the ground
Of native rock, two-story height
Massive and lovely, built so sound
It held the heat on winter nights

He added bedrooms upstairs soon
Small cozy spaces, so well made
A trailer served as extra room
For family and friends who stayed

He built a greenhouse then, and more
A room to hold his black and whites
A place to mat and frame and store
A fruit cellar dug down just right

A sunroom facing the south side
A darkroom helped him ply his art
A larger bedroom for a bride
A great room, near the home's new heart

He managed his woods from the start
Creating clearings, cutting weeds
Balsams especially, did their part
To fill his time with deadly deeds

A garden of perennials
Arranged to show the colors fine
And brighten up a wooded glade
With blooms all through the summertime

His efforts live in wood and soil
And those who know his history
The years passed quickly as he toiled
And left behind a legacy

A builder changes what he sees
With tangible and useful art
His hands both mind and heart do please
A monument from end to start

The poet too, has heart and mind
To sense it though, he must be read
More subtle meaning there to find
No matter he's alive or dead

THE WHISKER WOODSMAN

His whiskers spackled through with gray
As though he'd not washed up from work
His hair a little thin, they say
A floppy hat he does not shirk

Some people reckon he is tall
He seems so pictured in the woods
They judge him by the loads he hauls
Larger perhaps than most men would

A canvas canoe, not Kevlar
Duluth pack full of cooking gear
Heavy equipment toted far
And bulky canvas tent, I hear

He paddles spring and fall up north
Just after ice-out, before freeze
When biting flies do not go forth
In coldest water, stiffest breeze

He leaves the border lakes behind
For northern lands with caribou
Long portages are on his mind
An even trade for solitude

Others he welcomes in the woods
Who respect too the country's terms
And value nature as they should
As teacher from whom one can learn

His oven makes great bannock bread
Whiskerwood gives his fires a start
Dried out tinder from limbs long dead
The frazzled ends of wood or bark

In autumn when it's ricing time
Another use for his canoe
Ripe heads that nod when grain is prime
With ricing sticks he takes his due

And then a deer hunt on his land
No cabin there, just trusty tent
He doesn't even use a stand
Yet venison is his way sent

He winter-camps a week or two
Takes time from work when it is slack
His gear hauled in on sled, snowshoes
If it's too cold, he's too soon back

But lake trout may long hold him there
Deep in the Boundary Waters' wild
The fish are lively, and the air
Though weather doesn't pass for mild

Whatever he does, he does well
Through focus and persistence too
His outdoor skills are not to sell
But to be freely shared with you

The whisker woodsman ventures forth
From a small house he owns in town
When he's outdoors, he lives the north
The lakes and woods his only bounds

RUNNING AROUND

They say running is hard on knees
The rhythmic pounding, if you please
But cushioned soles absorb my weight
So I just shuffle to my fate

On gravel roads or grassy berms
I seek surfaces not too firm
Where terra firma has some give
I guess I run mostly to live

Life takes me to many places
Where I run, sometimes in races
I exercise, try hard to get
The feel of places not felt yet

Through Glacier Park, where I once worked
On mountainsides where grizzlies lurked
At Lake MacDonald, Iceberg too
Backcountry trails just right for youth

Past Arkansas' swamps and bayous
Dakota's prairies, potholes too
On Colorado's shortgrass plains
Up mountains high – splendor and pain

Through D.C.'s fine and famous mall
Near placid pool, monuments tall
In the Great Smoky's bluish haze
And Keys West, Largo and Biscayne

Up on the Kenai's dark cold roads
In Anchorage, past hookers bold
Near Thunder Bay's small creeks and woods
Alberta's ranch and city moods

In New York City's Central Park
With other crazies in the dark
Near Finger Lakes by fields of corn
Ithaca where Cornell was born

And along Baja's coastal slopes
On Santa Cruz, Galapagos
In New Zealand's historic towns
On Guam where war no longer sounds

'Round Kilauea's pungent rim
On Kona shores to stay in trim
Haleakala's xeric miles
Near Alawai with canoe trials

On San Antonio's River Walk
In Alpine, Texas near Sul Ross
And down in Tucson's sun-drenched heat
Past giant saguaros, at their feet

In old Xian, Beijing's empire
High-up Chongqing, busy Shanghai
Vancouver, B.C., early morn
Then some t'ai chi on wet grass lawns

Rochester streets, Mayo Clinic
By lakes and parklands, not the finish
And then here home at Eagles Nest
Sometimes, familiar trails are best

Ironic – running slows me down
Which helps me as I run around
To use my time to think and look
Perhaps create a poem or book

Or organize and plan ahead
Celebrate what I sense instead
Breathe the good air, enjoy the view
And give thanks for the old and new

ABOUT THE AUTHOR

Chuck Stone is a retired research biologist, with experience in many states during his work years. Born and raised in Minnesota, he has lived in the north since 1994, and near Ely since 2000. He has written or edited a number of scientific and popular works related to problem, rare and managed species of animals and plants and conservation biology, most recently in Hawai'i. Chuck has had a lifelong interest in the outdoors, and enjoys reading, theology, t'ai chi and music. This is his fourth published collection of poems.

ABOUT THE ARTIST

Jeff Kitterman is a biological illustrator, working primarily in pen and ink and utilizing various crosshatching techniques. Jeff began drawing living forms as an undergraduate at the University of Northern Iowa, and carried his interest forward as a teaching tool during his career as a secondary biology teacher in Iowa. Some of his influences have been Andrew Wyeth, Francis Lee Jaques, Philip Goodman and Roger Bateman. Attention to structural detail, textures and form define Jeff's technique. His studio and home is located in Sauk Centre, MN – visit www.jkdrawings.com for more information on Jeff's artwork.

RECENT BOOKS BY C. P. STONE

China: Impressions in Verse. 2007. A collection of haiku describing a first visit to China.

When I was a Kid. 2008. A collection of short poems about growing up in Minnesota in the 1940s.

Looking North: Images of Life in Northern Minnesota. 2009. A collection of haiku about a year in the north, season by season.

All published by and available through:

 Shadow IRIS Books
4451 Lakeside Drive
Eveleth, MN 55734-4400

or online at
www.speravi.com/irisbooks

WATCH FOR

Seeking the Needle at the Bottom of the Sea. A collection of short poems about trying to find wisdom in life experiences. Projected publication 2012.